When Anything Goes

WHEN ANYTHING GOES

Being Christian *in a* Post-Christian World

LESLIE
WILLIAMS

ABINGDON PRESS
NASHVILLE

WHEN ANYTHING GOES
BEING CHRISTIAN IN A POST-CHRISTIAN WORLD

Macro Editor: Jamie Clarke Chavez

Library of Congress Cataloging-in-Publication Data

Names: Williams, Leslie, 1951- author.
Title: When anything goes : being Christian in a post-Christian world / Leslie Williams.
Description: First [edition]. | Nashville, Tennessee : Abingdon Press, 2016. | Includes bibliographical references.
Identifiers: LCCN 2015049316 (print) | LCCN 2015049871 (ebook) | ISBN 9781630881269 (binding:pbk.) | ISBN 9781630881276 (E-book)
Subjects: LCSH: United States—Church history—21st century. | Christianity and culture—United States—History—21st century.
Classification: LCC BR526 .W5375 2016 (print) | LCC BR526 (ebook) | DDC 261.0973—dc23
LC record available at http://lccn.loc.gov/2015049316

16 17 18 19 20 21 22 23 24—10 9 8 7 6 5 4 3 2 1
MANUFACTURED IN THE UNITED STATES OF AMERICA

at the end of it all
we bow out
more or less gracefully
leaving
a vase of fierce flowers
on the altar—
a gift for whichever God
we knew best

—Leslie Williams

For Stockton,
my beloved

Contents

Note to the Reader

I LOVE SCHOLARLY WRITING. It's so safe. Every sentence is qualified, every thought is footnoted from a host of authorities, and the chances are excellent that you won't mortally offend your readers, even if your ideas are new or unconventional.

In this text, I have abandoned a scholar's voice. The reader will find no elaborate theories or theological jargon here. This book is parked in the dangerous intersection of theology, poetry, personal experience, and humor, so proceed with caution: *When Anything Goes* is about real life.

Introduction

Or What This Book Has to Do with Anything

In the 1950s Bible Belt, everyone I knew went to one church or another. The Baptists had the best Bible school, the Methodists had a great Sunday kids' program, the Catholics had special classes in catechism, but my family was Episcopalian. We had Thomas Cranmer's Book of Common Prayer, written in beautiful, poetic, sixteenth-century language—but incomprehensible (read: boring) to a child. At age five, I drew pictures on the pew bulletin, sitting next to my mother, who thunked me on my leg if I wiggled; the high point of the worship service was the parade of ladies' hats during the procession to the Communion rail. The mysterious veils, the silk flowers, the colorful hatbands—it was a feast for a young girl's eyes.

Over the next two decades, churchgoers lost the hats. Then, Episcopalians lost the old prayer book.

Finally, after half a century of church squabbles, secularism, and Sunday morning golf games, we lost the people, our congregation dwindling along with most other mainline denominations.

When I went back to school in the late 1980s at age thirty-seven to get a PhD in literature, I discovered that the world was now "post-Christian." Sophisticated and intelligent people no longer believed in the Judeo-Christian metanarrative or the Resurrection. I was surprised to find the situation so bad. I considered myself both a thinking person as well as a person of faith, and I didn't see a disconnect between brains and belief.

Then, in my fifties, I went to the East Coast to get a Masters of Sacred Theology, and I was surprised again—this time to learn that many post-Christian people had turned downright aggressive against Christians, dismissing traditional believers as if we wore outdated intellectual spats and whalebone corsets. Scorned, Christians were no longer with the program.

Wow. First the "God Is Dead" movement, now the "Beyond Christ" mentality. Western civilization has done a pretty thorough job of routing out Christianity from secular universities—and this is not to mention the masses of Americans who have simply floated away from the church on rafts of religious ennui or been lured by the enticing cultural distractions the world has to offer.

From an English professor's point of view, it seems we have produced a generation of young people who no longer understand Biblical references in literature—and who don't know what they are missing.

The description "post-Christian" is, actually, an accurate one, and started with our constitutional separation of Church and State. "Post-Christian" means that kings, princes, (and democratic governments) can't force people to kneel in Christian churches anymore; that our legislature can no longer base laws on Christian faith and Christian values; that Christian prayers cannot be spoken aloud in secular places, like schools; that sports groups can schedule soccer games on Sunday mornings; that stores are open on the Christian Sabbath; and that the steam engine of Christian morality no longer fuels our notions of right and wrong.

This description of post-Christianity accounts for the discrepancy between the general culture and our most reliable polls (Pew or Gallup, for example)—which claim that 70 percent of Americans are Christian believers. We live in an age in which Christianity is no longer the ocean everybody swims in, but faith is more like rivers, streams, and lakes on individual property. Still, I find it interesting that the current age has not come up with a new label for itself but defines itself in terms of what it has lost: the influence of Christianity.

The current age has not come up with a new label for itself but defines itself in terms of what it has lost: the influence of Christianity.

Western civilization may have declined, but individual belief still stands.

To attempt to write a Christian apology (a defense of the faith) in a "post-Christian" culture is an intimidating challenge, if for no other reason that, at first glance, such an apology seems to be looking backward to some sort of "Golden Age" of Christianity instead of looking forward to an exciting, emerging world—and Americans worship progress, not regress. No one likes to think their beliefs and ideas are "out of style."

Also, most apologies are written against a particular strain of cultural or theological viruses weakening the faith—against heresies, or against the replacement of faith by science, for instance. In a multicultural world, the choices of what to argue against are too many: against materialism, against relative morality, against religious apathy, against the dissolution of the nuclear family and the values it represented, against the global polarization of affluence/poverty, against the government, against the hegemony of political correctness, against fear of Muslim encroachment in the West, against advances in technology, medicine, science, and so forth.

Yet, Christianity speaks to every age, including this one, no matter what we label the age—and even if America thinks we have moved past the Christian era, with its myths, stuffy traditions, and nonscientific thinking. This book proposes to explore why God is anything but dead, why Jesus Christ has not been left by the side of the road, and why the Holy Spirit still breathes across the land of the free and the brave, saving us from our own prejudices and bad decisions.

Several books in the last few decades have argued the case for Christianity using different apologetic styles and approaches. This book is not so much a formal "apology" as an explanation, a distillation of my sixty-plus years of living in the American funhouse. I invite the reader to disagree with my ideas, to counter the rhetoric I use, and to refute the conclusions I've drawn from my reading and experience. However, since this book really isn't an argument, but a narrative, I also invite the reader to join me in your own journey.

1

I Was Not My Own Idea

By the work one knows the workman.
—Jean de la Fontaine

THE *DIVINE COMEDY* IS NOT JUST a foretaste of Hell for liars, thieves, and other lowlife types, but it also provides a compendium of all the scientific knowledge available in Dante's time, including the well-known, unassailable fact that the earth was the center of the universe. Some of the other prevailing scientific theories are almost humorous, like Dante's account of human reproduction, an explanation that makes any American fifth grader look smarter in terms of knowing how babies are made.

According to Dante—who is quoting the very latest scientific knowledge of his time—in the human male, thirsty veins drink up most of his healthy blood, sparing out a bit of special blood. As this special blood passes through the heart, it acquires the power to create human limbs. This blood is then re-digested and descends to the male's anatomical part better left unmentioned, where it is deposited into a natural receptacle. There, in the female, it mixes with her blood, coagulating and then quickening into a soul. At this point, the male's active virtue (from his perfect blood) labors in the inactive woman, and, like a sea sponge, a new human grows until birth.

And there you have it. Dante would have been astounded to learn about the microscopic goings on required to create a new human being. Sperm? Eggs? Not coagulated blood? He would have been even more shocked to discover that the genesis of life can actually be accomplished in a Petri dish. I personally know several healthy, happy, intelligent human beings who got their start in a laboratory and were brought to term in a woman who had nothing to do with their conception.

Science, of course, has changed since Dante's time, along with the rest of Dante's cultural assumptions. When reading any landmark author, it's helpful to know a few facts about his culture and how the culture shapes the work. For instance, in Dante's time, the Vatican was the hub of power for religious life, with a hierarchy of minions who patrolled every word spoken by kings and peasants alike. Vying for political power, the Emperor fought the Pope for centuries in fierce and bloody battles. Women were either goddesses or doormats possessed by a male sibling, husband, or father; and the poets revered courtly love, which meant that eye contact was about the only contact Dante ever had with the love of his life, Beatrice—although she is his heavenly inspiration through thirty-three cantos of world-famous poetry.

In general, culture is the sea of shifting tides and currents in which we live and move and have our being. While immersed, we can't see the invisible water channels that tug us, propel us, push against us—or avoid the riptide that is likely to carry us far from our umbrellas on the beach. Prophets try to post warning signs where the currents are dangerous; but prophets can be killed, ignored—or voted out of office.

Our family in the 1950s thrived in the American cultural ocean. My parents threw cocktail parties and patio barbeques at our new house, where people drank and smoked to their hearts' content (ignorant of the condition of their livers and lungs). Both the economy and the number of babies were booming. My father wore a suit to work every day in an oil company, while my mother stayed at home, went to garden club, sewing club, and volunteered at church. Children of the Great Depression, our parents promoted hard work as the key to success ("do your homework!"), combined with frugality (counting toilet paper squares). "Be nice" was the watchword for all Southern girls, and, of course, everybody went to church.

Jumping ahead fifty years, my family of origin did not survive intact, contributing to the skyrocketing divorce statistics, as America stampeded through women's liberation, the sexual revolution, the Vietnam War, and the invasion of the drug cartels. Further, the new millennium has brought terrorism, political correctness with a vengeance, a rash of children raised by single mothers with different baby daddies, custody battles, and multimillion-dollar lawsuits about hot coffee.

And technology! I watched my grandbaby, Evelyn, not yet two and still in diapers, sitting on our couch, playing—and winning—a "shapes and colors" game on her mother's cell phone. Too much has already been written about the way Facebook, tweets, and FaceTime have affected friendships and communication, how technology has changed the way we play games, and how it has spawned abuses like easy access to child porn and Trojan horses.

A generalized Higher Power hovers benevolently over our lives, and deities from multicultural faiths spread before the spiritually hungry like an all-you-can-eat religious restaurant. These days—in art, fashion, lifestyle, manners, behavior, and religion—anything goes.

If I'm going to explain why I'm a Christian swimming against the post-Christian American cultural currents, I have to use reasoning that works in this day and age and not logic from the past. For example, I can't say, "I believe in Jesus because the Bible tells me so"; no, in the general culture, the Bible no longer carries the authority it used to. I can't say, "The universe was created by God" because the existence of God is what's in question. I can't even toss around the words *soul* or *truth* because post-modernism has claimed there is no absolute truth, that all "truth" is relative. Objectivity is obsolete. And we have no soul, no center, no self, but are made up of mere echoes from tradition, from brain chemistry, and from our past experience.

Other things to consider include the notion of "sin," which we've jettisoned in favor of defining evil in terms of a bad choice, a psychological problem, a hormone imbalance, a disease, an abused childhood—and, whenever possible, somebody else's fault.

Advertising has convinced us that we, as entitled people, deserve all the goodies the world can give us. Enough of the right material things will satisfy us as human beings.

Finally, as books, newspapers, and the Internet tell us, science is king. If it can't be measured or proven, it is superstition or otherwise dubiously real.

So I'll have to start my story from scratch. At this point, I also need to confess that this examination of the faith is not merely an intellectual exercise for me. After half a century of Christian belief, and after a quarter century of being married to an Episcopal priest, I have hit a bump in the road in a particular area of my life. I can no longer take faith, or God, or the Bible for granted. It's time for a seasoned reexamination.

I don't believe doubt is a bad thing. If we're honest with ourselves, most of us have had moments when we wonder if the whole shebang is for real, or if we're crazy. Here's my position at this point in my life: if Jesus Christ is real, then He will hold up under close examination. In fact, any Person or belief that we give our hearts, minds, bodies, souls to deserves (and requires) close scrutiny.

If, as Glenda of Oz says, "It's always best to start at the beginning," then I suppose a look at the creation of the universe is in order before addressing individual beginnings. When I was five, I learned that our sun was not really yellow, the way we see it. The sun was really a huge red-orange ball of molten and exploding fire. The next day at kindergarten, I sat down in my miniature chair at the drawing table and colored a flamboyant picture of a huge red sun. My teacher asked, "What is that you're drawing in the sky?"

I replied, "It's the sun."

"Why is it red?"

"Because I found out that the sun is really a big red ball of fire!"

My teacher responded firmly, "Even if that's true, you need to color your sun yellow."

The incident served as my introduction to cosmology—and to the notion that most people (even adults) believe only what they see.

At age seven, I proudly rattled off the names of the planets to my parents and anyone who would listen; at nine, I learned about galaxies and stars and the universe. I used to look up at the constellations in the night sky, awed, but then turn my eyes back to the things that mattered in my busy life as a kid, things like collecting rocks, jumping double rope, and learning how to tap dance. The universe was background music, pleasant but vague.

Then Stephen Hawking published *A Brief History of Time* in 1988 and torpedoed God's seven-day creation spree as the culture's dominant creation narrative.

I'm not a scientist, so my understanding of physics is simple and basic. Apparently, the universe began as a tiny speck, intensely hot and dense, that appeared out of nowhere, out of nothing. Scientists call this tiny particle a "singularity," like the dense gravitational forces at the bottom of black holes.

In one moment over thirteen billion years ago, this singularity exploded—or expanded as many scientists prefer to say—creating the universe. After the initial expansion, the universe cooled enough to allow energy to convert into subatomic particles, protons, neutrons, and electrons. Hydrogen along with traces of helium and lithium were the first elements produced, and giant clouds of these primordial components coalesced through gravity to form stars and galaxies. This beginning of matter brought with it the beginning of time and space.

The Big Bang is the new favored creation story, buttressed by the latest technological evidence and scientific theories.

Here's where it gets interesting. The speck received some sort of push to become activated, some kind of momentum, but scientists know nothing about "before" the sudden expansion. In what context did the singularity appear if space, time, matter, and energy did not yet exist? The most renowned physicists in the field don't know. The folks at *All About Science* say, "We don't know where it came from, why it's here, or even where it is. All we really know is that we are inside of it and at one time it didn't exist and neither did we." Our bodies are made, literally, of stardust, elements from exploded stars, elements that exist on earth. Dust. But why did the speck appear? Where did it come from? What momentum caused it to expand in one specific instant?

I find the Big Bang theory fascinating. I also find it fascinating—although it's not commonly mentioned—that scientists will admit that the Big Bang theory is not the only current scientific theory about the origins of the universe. Yes, the Big Bang theory is based on the latest scientific observations, but as leading British scientist George F. R. Ellis admitted in *Scientific American*, there are a range of other models that could explain the scientific observations of the last decades, including a "spherically symmetrical universe with Earth at the center, and you cannot disprove it based on observation."

So we have a theory of how the universe was created, a theory generated from data we have observed through high tech equipment, but even the leading scientists have many unanswered questions.

To make matters even more interesting, according to a family friend who happens to be an astronomer, Dr. Bobby Ulich, we are not dealing with a mere single universe when we ponder cosmology, but many universes—*multi*-verses—which is an even more staggering proposition.

Human study of the origins of the universe resembles a bunch of brilliant infants playing with a Rubik's Cube—bright and colorful and good to teethe on, but way, way, way beyond our scope of understanding. We are frogs, hopping around the pond without really much of a clue how the pond came to be. Even if we are armed with the latest knowledge about the beginnings of the universe, how does one examine either the presence or the necessity of God?

The human race has been so eager to understand the origin of life and the universe that throughout history we have jumped with relish on the latest, hottest evidence that proves whatever theory is current—a theory that, more often than not, is disproved by further evidence and another new theory. Look at how naive medieval science looks today. What will our theories look like in the next five centuries?

Perhaps we should look at the human need for proof instead of for the proof itself. Do we feel that more knowledge gives us more control?

Actually, the Big Bang theory and the biblical story of creation have several things in common. First, scientists admit that before the appearance of the "singularity" (the tiny speck that contained the universe), there was "nothing"—or rather there was an unknown "before." In the Genesis account, God created the universe out of nothing, *ex nihilo*. Both biblical creationists and scientists agree that there was a determinable, measurable Beginning—that eternity, space, time, and the earth didn't exist before creation.

Actually, the Big Bang theory and the biblical story of creation have several things in common.

I have a hard enough time with statistics like the one I heard the other day on the radio: Road Runner was the first mega supercomputer system that could process a quadrillion mathematical calculations per second. A quadrillion calculations per second!! As amazing as that statistic is, it is still countable, finite. But I simply can't wrap my mind around the notion that there was no "before" the Beginning. Part of my brain thinks it needs to understand "before" if I'm going to understand "after." Both the biblical account and the Big Bang theory inspire awe because my mind isn't constructed to comprehend a "nothingness" before the start of matter, time, and space.

In the face of my limited intellectual ability, I'm forced to admit that there's a power, a mighty energy force out there that's a whole lot smarter than I am. But what to call this Something? Some scientists call this Something "God," but it's a "God" with different characteristics than the biblical God.

Two heavyweights thrash out this question: Nobel laureate Steven Weinberg claims that the Being that emerges from scientific investigation should be called an "abstract principle of order and harmony," and not labeled with a word like "God," because the word *God* is loaded with emotional, historical, and spiritual connotations. After all, he says, "the more the universe seems comprehensible, the more it also seems pointless," and the use of the word *God* implies meaning.

On the other end of the argument is Australian biologist Charles Birch, who gleans from the same scientific observations: "I find meaning in it."

So, ultimately, we have a choice to make. Scientists and Creationists agree that a larger Being, a Force, a Something created the universe and kicked off space/time as we know it. The choice involves the label we give this Something. We can call it "God" or not. And what we call this Being includes our conception of this Being's intentions in creating the universe in the first place. We can look at the available information for ourselves and decide whether it holds meaning for us or not.

Both the Big Bang theory and the biblical account of creation have other similarities, but neither extreme fundamentalism nor hard-core scientific inquiry advertises this connection. No matter what we choose to believe, we are beggars looking at a queen. Whether the sovereign is personal and kind, or cold and distant, we cannot deny the evidence that humans didn't create the universe. And we didn't create ourselves. We may think we're smart, but no human being alive can create something out of nothing.

Finally, the Big Bang theory, like the theory of evolution, is a theory. As I teach my rhetorical analysis students, be sure to distinguish between theories, opinions, and facts when you are making a point. If I am going to choose to believe in the Christian God, it is senseless to get my knickers in a twist over scientific theories that—like Dante's solar system—could easily be disproved in the next hundred years.

In comparing the biblical account of creation and scientific evidence, the issue of time comes up—six days over and against thirteen billion years. Time, it seems, is another thorny issue. Time is related to speed. As Dr. Ulich says, time is relative according to Einstein. "To an outside observer, a clock that travels at a high relative 'speed' appears to progress more slowly."

In other words, a clock on the earth and an identical clock on the moon would seem to keep time differently. Scientists did an experiment with three clocks set with matching times. One clock, located at the United States Naval Observatory, circled on the surface of the earth as it revolved. A second clock revolved around the earth in a 707 flying at ten kilometers above the earth. A third clock revolved around the earth in the Concord flying at twenty kilometers. When the clocks came back together, three different times were measured.

The original *Planet of the Apes* and, more recently, *Interstellar* illustrate this principle. The spaceship takes off from earth and returns to earth, but time on earth has passed at a faster rate than time in the spaceship. The international date line is another indicator of the variance in time. A person can take off one day and land in yesterday (although the date line is a practical solution for the difference in the earth's time and has nothing to do with the theory of relativity).

Six days versus thirteen billion years sounds like an enormous discrepancy. However, given the wrinkles that time presents and the vastness of the universe, I'm not going to bet the ranch on this dispute. The argument is, in a way, a false argument because absolute understanding of time and its measurement (in spite of Einstein) is just beyond the grasp of human comprehension. In light of these thoughts, science for me does not cancel out the Bible.

At any rate, as I lie out on the hood of my car, looking up at the night sky, I see myself as a tiny speck of dust living on a larger speck of dust in a reality far beyond my grasp, and I am grateful to the Being who made it possible.

Just as science doesn't cancel out faith in terms of the creation of the universe, science also doesn't supersede belief in terms of our beginnings as a species. Science and the Bible coincide with the discovery of a Mitochondrial Eve, the mother of all humans. Some scientists argue that this matrilineal ancestor doesn't "prove" the biblical story, but science is not finished exploring this issue, either. Besides, the Bible itself relates two different stories of the creation of human beings, Genesis 1:1–2:3, and Genesis 2:4-25.

Here's the question: Seeing babies lined up like flower buds in the hospital nursery—is each one the result of random chance or are we individually designed by a God who fashioned us when we were still in the sloshy, safe, darkness of our mother's womb?

My own mother miscarried the baby she had conceived three months before me. When she showed signs of miscarrying me as well, the doctor said, "We'll let this one go and I'll give you drugs to keep the next one."

My mother responded, "No. Give me the drugs now. I want to keep this one." I picture my mother lying for weeks against a white bank of down pillows surrounded by her iced tea, milkshakes, magazines, and bottles of pills—and as a result of the drugs and bed rest, I entered the world six months later. I often think of my existence as a miracle, helped along by my mother, the doctor, and the latest medication.

My Ob-Gyn claims that all babies are miracles. Strictly speaking, a miracle is an event that can't be explained, and we can now explain how life is conceived and brought to term. The number of miracles has nosedived in direct proportion to the increase in scientific knowledge. So maybe *miracle* isn't the right word.

In the field of medicine, like the field of physics, stuff still happens that we can't explain. Why do "miracle" drugs heal some people and not others? In the process of conception and birth, it takes millions of sperm attacking the egg, gnawing away at the egg's outer layer, to make it thin enough for one sperm to penetrate and combine its DNA with the egg's DNA.

This we know. However, though science is working on it, we can't yet rig the lotto system to predict which of the millions of sperm will be the winner. We can call conception a random microscopic event, or we can call it a miracle; either way, we can't explain why that particularly hardy sperm beat the crowd.

Considering all the possibilities my biological parents had to offer, I could have been a much different person if a different little DNA swimmer had won the race—blonde instead of dark, short instead of tall, good with numbers instead of a mathematical idiot... the list goes on and on. I did not get to pick my DNA package. Besides, it was not my idea to be born in the first place.

To complicate matters, every existence is dependent on millennia of encounters, dinner parties, and blind dates as my ancestors met each other. I know it's become a romance novel cliché, but it's true in my case: if a particular young woman hadn't married a specific Scottish carriage maker in the sixteenth century, I would not be writing these words today. And you are reading these words under the same phenomenon of circumstance.

When my husband and I started trying to have children, we discovered that the miracle so common to the rest of our friends wasn't going to happen to us, in spite of three surgeries and a host of drugs that threatened to give me facial hair, drugs so strong they made the sidewalk lines jiggle, drugs that could have given us quintuplets—drugs that worked for other women but not for me. Modern science failed us.

God failed us.

In all, I lost eighty-four babies, spent eighty-four bouts of sadness curled up under a down comforter with a heating pad. Eighty-four imaginary babies swirling down the drain of my imagination. Seven and a half years of prayers answered no. Not to mention the pain of reading abortion statistics (all those dead, inchoate lives and we couldn't jump-start a new human being no matter what we did). We watched unplanned bundles of extra trouble appear in the lives of our friends like cabooses attached to their family plans.

Then one phone call, and our caseworker at the Gladney Center for Adoption placed a precious baby boy in our arms—a tiny, soft bundle, his face furled in sleep. Three years later, we received a beautiful baby girl with dimples like grape seeds, also from Gladney.

Did God play a role in the creation and the birth of our children? Can we attribute the receipt of two gifts of new life to a caring Being who heard our pleas? Or was it all a coincidence?

Our son's birth mother was a Roman Catholic who chose not to abort her child. Our daughter's birth mother was an Episcopalian who requested an active Episcopal family for her baby.

I had to rethink my relationship with the Being I called God. These two cooing, squirming babies were so right for us, smiling up at us with toothless delight. Handpicked, it seemed. The joy I felt rocking them in our antique family rocker helped me overcome my cynicism and doubt. The facts surrounding my own birth, our children's birth stories—a pattern? Could I connect the God of the universe with this life-giving force who created my children and me?

In the construction of a theology that can hold its head up in the twenty-first century, I choose to believe that the Being who created the universe had a hand in creating me and my children. This Being is a life-giving force. I don't know why my mother miscarried the child before me, why children are born with defects, why children are born and neglected.

Somebody created the universe—and that same Somebody cares about the individuals living on our speck of dust.

For now, what makes the most sense in terms of both science and my life experience is that Somebody created the universe—and that same Somebody cares about the individuals living on our speck of dust. For me, not only is this belief more comforting than belief in a rolling of cosmic dice, but I am choosing to call this Being "God."

2

I'm Addicted to Meaning

Life is not primarily a quest for pleasure, as Freud believed,
or a quest for power, as Alfred Adler taught,
but a quest for meaning.
—Harold Kushner

I NEVER HAD A TOOTH CAVITY UNTIL I was thirty-six years old. Then my dentist told me I had nine. My teeth had rotted overnight. The upshot of this alarming discovery was that I faced an entire day at the dentist's office.

On the big day while I was still in the lobby, the dentist gave me a pill I'd never heard of, Halcion. Ten minutes later, he and my husband dragged me into the office and together poured me into the chair; then the dentist started drilling. That day, I remember discussing with him a surgical operation I'd had three years prior, going into the gory details, spouting way too much information to share with your dentist (or anybody else for that matter).

At the next visit, I apologized all over myself. The dentist looked at me and smiled. "Don't worry. You never said a word to me all day."

"Oh, but I remember clearly. Telling you all about—"

"No. I promise. The drug I gave you—well, it's pretty strong."

Stunned, I thought, *That conversation was as real to me as this one is.* Was the whole thing inside my head? What a terrifying thought.

The subject of reality came up two months ago, when I was at lunch with a group of friends. As we sat around the table at the Copper Kitchen, someone suggested that our reality is our thoughts. We ARE our thoughts, which led to a whole slew of questions:

Were we sitting at the Copper Kitchen sharing a reality of spinach salad, enchiladas, and chocolate cake, or was this lunch experience simply in the mind of each of us?

Were we figments of each others' imaginations?

What if a person diagnosed with paranoid schizophrenia or Alzheimer's were eating lunch with us? Who would decide which reality is more real?

What if the definition of reality simply means believing our own inner propaganda? (For example, if we think we're sniveling, we're sniveling. If we think we're strong, we're strong.)

If this last definition is true, then the good news is that most of us aren't stuck in a miserable reality. We can move from sniveling to strong. Repeating "I think I can, I think I can, I think I can" can lead to a shift in reality. In other words, we can convert stinking thinking into positive vibes.

So how does a change in reality occur? Methods of transformation vary in effectiveness: (1.) hallucinogenic drugs (quick but weird and temporary), (2.) electrical brain shocks (popular way back when, but today—not so much), (3.) lobotomy (extreme), (4.) retraining the brain pathways Pavlovian style (works well but takes awhile), (5.) retraining the brain pathways using new technology (still experimental), (6.) psychotherapy or counseling (good or not, depending on the therapist), (7.) Moving across the country (a temporary fix because emotional and mental baggage tends to cling like a rucksack superglued to the skin of our backs), (8.) medication (excellent if you get the right meds, disastrous if you don't), and (9.) hanging with a more encouraging crowd (always a good choice).

Certain mental illnesses and severe personality disorders aside, creating a meaningful personal reality starts with the desire to do so and the belief that you can. The ability to cope, to overcome, to relinquish pain, to turn suffering into joy is available more often than not. But we have to want it. Badly.

Freedom of choice penetrates deep in the American psyche. Most of us were breast-fed on the "can-do" attitude. Americans will fight to the death for our right to choose anything—from what action to take at a major life junction to which canned spaghetti we prefer.

In fact, American life is infested with a different problem that's grown exponentially in the last fifty years. We used to drink water from the tap or the well. Now, we all know what a trip to any supersized grocery store brings—either paralysis of over-choice (standing in front of the bottled water section, staggered by the selection), or else, once we've made our choice, suffering from the side effects: maybe I should have bought the artificially flavored water instead of purified or natural or carbonated. Or no bottled water at all.

We are continually distracted from the lions in life, because we are covered with swarms of ants, stinging us for our attention.

Choice. My mother-in-law, a brilliant former state district judge, announced with conviction on her eighty-third birthday in 2011 that the current year was 1984—and in her reality of progressive dementia, it was. Yet earlier, even as she was sliding into the twilight of her intellect, she said, "I've never been so happy." At peace with herself and the world, she was watching cartoons on television at the time. Though she seemed to understand what was happening to her, she chose to accept it.

Or two hypothetical motorcyclists have accidents and break their necks. One chooses to smoke himself to death—the only movement he can make is to inhale in his bed. The other decides to live with hope and becomes an inspiration to those around him.

Again, choice.

The intellectual gurus today tell us that the past is fiction—or at best, a distorted look through the wacky glasses of the present. For example, every World War II movie made is as much about the culture it was produced in as it is about the years between 1940 and 1945. In fact, I wrote my dissertation on narratives based on earlier texts, exploring the ways literature has chosen to rewrite the past in a current interpretation.

A slippery business, reality. Take the memories of any given family vacation. The son says, "Remember the time Susie caught the big fish in Estes Park? Then she fell in the water. She was, like, four years old." Susie pipes up, "No, I fell in the water two years later. When I was four, Dad had to reel the fish in because I was too little." Dad adds, "Wait. It wasn't Estes Park, it was Boulder." Mom chimes in, "No, it wasn't Estes

Park or Boulder. It was Lyons, and I made cheese sandwiches. Susie soaked hers when she fell in."

I rest my case.

Since we've defenestrated objective reality, (literally in French, throwing it out the window), the closest we can get these days is a "consensual" reality. My friends at the Copper Kitchen agreed that, yes, we were sharing the same reality.

Big scale or small, the lack of a consensual reality causes mayhem, misunderstandings, and murder. If free love is included in one spouse's reality but not the other's, a divorce is likely. If one country wants another country's land (or power or trade routes or *lebensraum* or whatever the country's power structure thinks it's entitled to in its collective reality) war breaks out. The lack of consensual reality feeds psychiatrists, pays police officers, fuels the court system, and supports the military.

And governments. On the one hand, you have Hitler's "consensual" reality, consensual because it was enforced with murder, terror, and lies. Only a few dared to live a different reality. On the other hand, democracy has provided the fairest system of consensual reality, yet in any given election, as many as 49 percent of the people can be unhappy with the agreed-on reality. But at least the majority concur that you shouldn't haul off and kill all the people on the other side. We call this progress.

So what goes into the mix of creating a meaningful personal reality? What's in the Self that we construct? Context. IQ. Family. Gifts. Flaws. DNA. Circumstances. Luck. Some fixtures and furniture come with the room; some we collect as we go along. And in this room, what movies do we play on the wall? A critical mother scolding us? Visions of our dreams?

The trick to creating a meaningful reality is to learn how to pick and water the right plants that decorate the inner room. My father was an alcoholic and verbally intimidating. I kept his words like noxious plants lined up inside me, watering the bad memories. I finally reached the point in my life where I had to choose whether to keep irrigating the bitter recollections or to plant healthier trees to yield good fruit for my future. So I started a whole new garden.

We all know this truth, but it bears reminding: it's dangerous to judge ourselves from the inside, but others from the outside. Some people look like trees overloaded with perfect fruit. How easy life is for them! Not necessarily so. Creating a meaningful *inside* reality is the goal, and depends largely on grafting (applying others' advice), fertilizing (using the manure of life in a productive way), timing (waiting for the right moment), and learning to weather the storms.

Both my children went through the "why" stage when they were young, toddling around the house after me, asking strings of questions: "Why does Whisker the hamster always try to get out of his cage?" "Why can't we go swimming when it's raining?" "Why do you make me clean up my room?" "Why can't we have ice cream for supper?"

Little knee-high human beings, rooting around in their world for meaning. Bigger human beings follow the same process—except the questions are different: "Why don't you love me?" "Why am I alive?" "Why am I stuck in this dead-end job?" "Why did my brother-in-law die of cancer?"

Like food gathering, the search for meaning is part of our human DNA and necessary for survival. I can't imagine life without the quest for meaning—I might as well be Whisker, the hamster. Socrates called it the unexamined life—and also mentioned that it wasn't worth living.

The difference between the words "purpose" and "meaning"

is subtle but important. Purpose is the drive; meaning is the result. To use a fishing metaphor, the purpose of commercial ocean fishing is to catch a product to sell or eat. For the fisherman, the purpose of fishing is to earn money to survive. Meaning is the catch, the fish, the product of the purpose, and the satisfaction it brings to the fisherman.

Purpose and meaning are, of course, directly related. I don't go fishing and expect to find diamonds in the nets. I don't become a jeweler and expect to sell fish. I don't become a teacher and expect to find either fish or jewels sitting in the desks. In the metaphor of our chosen reality, we all have to make sure that the purpose and the meaning match. Otherwise, we're disappointed, and it feels as if life has no meaning.

We are programmed to search for meaning.

Unfortunately, life offers a myriad of meaning-killer opportunities. I may choose to be a fisherman, but there are days when the net comes up empty. Or, times when a loved one dies or a job is lost. Any number of thwarted goals can suck the meaning right out of a strong and righteous purpose.

Because life offers so many opportunities for failed dreams, it's easy to fall into Nietzsche's philosophy of nihilism. Nihilism is a chimera of a doctrine, popular for decades toward the end of the twentieth century. Nihilism squelches life's buoyancy. Nihilism rejects reality, denies existence, proclaims pointlessness. Nihilism is Eeyore to the max. One of the heads of nihilism, Deconstructionism, was the rage when I was in graduate school getting a PhD in literature. Using this method of literary analysis (in a broad sense), literature had no meaning, the texts made no sense, the author had died, the reader could read anything he or she wanted into a senseless story, and the purpose of everything was to proclaim that Nothing in Life Has Meaning.

As Wayne Booth in *The Rhetoric of Fiction* pointed out at the beginning of this epidemic of nothingness, the correct response to nihilism is suicide. Yet students in art, literature, philosophy, and religion flooded graduate schools, eager to get up cheerfully every morning and help contribute to the meaninglessness of life while savoring their cups of cappuccino.

As for me, when I had moved from the doctoral program at Baylor where I started a PhD and moved to the University of Houston's PhD program, I finally learned to play the Deconstruction game. But it was just a game. After discussing the meaninglessness of my favorite novels, I enjoyed going home to relish life with my husband, my two adorable babies, friends, tennis matches, and a neighborhood swimming pool.

HOWEVER, the rich and delicious meaning in this season of life came AFTER the first three years in Houston, when I spent many nights on the couch wrestling with fear, misery, and, yes, meaninglessness. Eleven family members died during this period, we lost our shirts on a house, our second child was a year late in arriving, and what was I doing in a PhD program, anyway?

Looking back through the crystal lens of 20/20 vision, I see that the last two years in Houston wouldn't have been so special if I hadn't suffered through the first three to find meaning in the misery.

Fatalists sport bumper stickers that proclaim: "Life is short, and then you die."

True. And yet.

We are programmed to search for meaning, in spite of apparent disasters—even though many of us at one time or another have been tempted to say, "Forget it. Death can't be worse than this." I am alive and writing these words, and if you are reading this, you are also alive, which means that you have opted to keep excavating for significance, digging for those emeralds embedded in the dirt and rock of experience. Old habits die hard, and suicide is one answer—but not the only (and certainly not the best) answer—to despair.

When I was two years old, I remember having a Little Golden Book, *The Little Engine That Could*, with the image of a colorful and cheery choo choo on the cover. For some reason, I became convinced that the cover picture hid another picture underneath, and I began to tear at the corner of the cardboard cover—which revealed, of course, only pressed gray material of the book's inexpensive construction.

My mother was cooking supper in the kitchen, bathed in a bright yellow light against an early darkening outside the window. She saw me destroying my favorite book and stopped me. I couldn't convince her that there was another picture underneath the cover.

The incident was an early lesson in meaning, from which I gleaned several life insights once I became an adult and looked back. First, early on significance was important, and I started probing underneath the obvious for something special.

Second, sometimes the meaning is right in front of you. You don't have to destroy something you love to find it.

Third, though meaning may be staring you in the face, sometimes it's not the answer you thought it would be. I thought the deeper meaning lay beneath the cover, but the deeper meaning had already implanted itself in my psyche. As a personality trait, the little choo choo's persistence has often motivated me beyond the realm of sanity and against great odds to succeed in a far-fetched dream.

Fourth, in examining this memory decades later, I learned that it sometimes takes years (like sixty or so) to figure out what you're looking for.

This final insight is a perspective that kids facing the great lake of the future have trouble achieving. However, any veteran of life—regardless of age—can look back and see incidents (usually painful) that have hardened into meaning, emerging like stepping stones across the great lake to help us get across. (Most old hands at living also see themselves struggling in the lake, trying to make it to the next rock, afraid to drown, but determined to keep going.)

Before birth, babies' brains produce trillions of nerve cells (as well as the connectors from cell to cell)—more than twice what we will need, and more brain cells than stars in the Milky Way. As soon as the cold air, fluorescent glare, and the delivery room's racket assault our brand-new bodies, our lungs let out a wail of protest over this new situation. The brain cells begin connecting to each other in networks.

Immediately, the baby's brain starts to figure out what this condition called "birth" means. Do I have to cry now and work my mouth to get my tummy full? I hear a familiar voice, but it's louder, and contact with my skin feels different, drier. Life is much harsher.

The quest for meaning starts at birth, long before we're conscious of it, as the brain cells crank into action. Each neuron cell looks like a tall tree with roots. The trunk is the axon, the branches are the dendrites, and the roots are the terminals. Like a lightning rod conducting electricity, impulses create pathways, connecting branches, trunks, and roots across synapses. Chemicals called neurotransmitters facilitate the impulse through the network of pathways. If the network isn't used, it disappears.

What this means for the baby is that early stimulation creates the pathways for life. Loving stimulation, hugs, and kisses influence the wiring of the brain, creating strong and healthy pathways. Bad experiences also shape a child's developing brain. Stress produces the hormone cortisol, which can cause some of the brain cells to die.

I like to think of the brain like Rocky Mountain National Park, filled with trees in dense forests and well-worn hiking trails snaking up and down though the deep ravines and staggering, rocky heights. Getting off the established path requires courage, determination, and a willingness to explore. But, like changing our thinking patterns, it can be done. Neuroplasty is an emerging field exploring the rerouting in the brain.

Every thought releases chemicals. Although Carl Sagan coined the term "wonder junkie," Jason Silva, host of National Geographic's *Brain Games,* discusses what happens in the brain to cause addiction to wonder, exploration, and discovery: dopamine influx.

> Dopamine is associated with seeking—it's not serotonin, it's not empathy, it's not the love drug.... It's driven toward the new. The new and the novel. That's why if you're in your room—you live in your room—everything becomes invisible. But you can always spot something that's different in your room. Or when you go to a new city, it's the reason why you feel, just, high! Why, all of a sudden, the most mundane... things are magic!

My personal operating thesis is that if dopamine—the feel-good chemical released in the brain—is associated with seeking, then the very search for meaning is rewarded with a high, whether we find what we're looking for or not. Spotting something different in the ordinary room of my life—and figuring out how it fits in with the rest of the décor—is just as good as a drug.

New additions to experience can be fantastic, but on the other hand, they can also be traumatic, like the car crash that killed my aunt. The brain immediately secretes negative chemicals with the stress of bad news. Yet sooner or later in the process of grief, the brain begins trying to figure out why the bad thing happened, and what the bad thing means.

Unfortunately, there is no magic formula for transforming the worm of misery into the butterfly of meaning. Sometimes people get stuck in the search. Sometimes the negative chemicals keep surging (post-traumatic stress disorder), but most of the time, the brain is able to assimilate the new and terrible thing into the larger structure of a person's value system. Searching for meaning is a bit like being a botanist who runs across a new plant and examines it from every angle until it can be classified within the larger order.

Given that human beings are constructed with the ability (and the necessity) of seeking to create order out of what feels like the random chaos of life, at some point the search for meaning becomes conscious and intentional. In the "hippie era" when I came of age, we called it "finding ourselves." My generation blew the lid off the search for meaning with psychedelic drugs on one end of the spectrum and transcendental meditation on the other, along with the sexual revolution, music riddled with hidden messages, and protest rallies that changed the establishment. Or so we hoped.

When none of the above satisfied the itch to find the deepest meaning of our lives, we grew older, our energy petered out, and eventually we became the establishment. Now we're telling our grandchildren the same things our parents told us: drive cautiously, save money, and get a good education.

Not that they'll listen. We certainly didn't. When it comes to finding meaning, every single one of us has to stick our own finger in the fan. I would like to know if there is even one parent out there who has told a teenager not to drive too fast and gotten this response. "What a great idea! Since you have more experience and wisdom than I do, I'll always stay within the speed limit."

Right.

My daughter loved to cook with me from an early age. When she was five, she learned the meaning of a hot coil on the stove, and why I kept telling her, "Don't touch." We just can't take anybody else's word for it.

The search for meaning is like eating a giant artichoke. We pull off leaf after leaf, each one with a thorny point on top and a little piece of the meat, which we sweep through the sauce of life and swallow, circling the artichoke deeper and deeper, until we get to the heart—covered with prickly bristles. Only after we scrape away the protective thistles do we get to the delicious center of it all.

With each bite of life, we get a bit of understanding, but most of our experiences come with a prick as well as sweetness. Sooner or later, we reach the heart of the matter and can no longer avoid the question: "What the heck are we doing on this planet? What is the purpose of existence?"

When I was seven years old, my mother tucked my sister and me into our matching twin beds in the blue room with patterned wallpaper. In early spring, a cool breeze flowed through the open window as the evening turned to night. My first inkling of something important beyond what I could see came as I played with my Raggedy Ann in the twilight, unable to sleep. Twirling the rag doll, I watched my arm, a skinny, freckled little piece of myself with soft, light hairs. My arm. I stared at my arm, touched it, looking at it in a new way. How did this piece of flesh get to be my arm? Where did it come from? Where did I come from? How did I come to be seven years old, lying in my bed?

With no answers, I fell asleep, awakening the next day to bacon and eggs for breakfast, a spelling test at school, and hopscotch at recess. The question came up again as a friend and I sat in her yellow convertible our senior year in college, eating Arby's roast beef sandwiches. What was going to happen after graduation? The discussion centered around what we wanted to do with our lives, skirting the issue of who we were going to be. The unspoken—and far more terrifying—question was why were we on the earth in the first place?

Four short years later, I had ruined everything. My marriage had tanked. I had begun the long, hard road of rejections from publishers. My family of origin had disintegrated. My closest friends lived six hours away, my sisters were as lost as I was, and I was barely speaking to my father.

Why? Why? Why? What was the point of any of it? Crying in a pink-tiled shower with a matching shower curtain, the water ran cold before a phrase from my childhood weaseled itself into a brain muddy with despair: "Give your life to Jesus."

Not exactly like the lights of Times Square, but a tiny birthday-sized candle flickered in a very dark place, then threatened to go out. Jesus, you see, had been the problem all along. My father had been a religious leader, and although he helped a great many people through his books and ministry, at home he was not attentive to how his behavior affected us. I did NOT want to give my life to Jesus, or be any more intimately involved in Christianity than attending a nice, proper Episcopal church on occasion. My father had forced me into Young Life, church groups, Christian camps—you name it, cramming Jesus down my throat since his own conversion when I was a child.

The last thing I wanted was to give Jesus control of my life.

Standing naked and shivering as the water swirled down the drain, I had to admit that twenty-five was really too young to be wishing the show were over. When I looked at things with the smidgen of objectivity I had left, I also had to admit that I'd done a pretty spectacular job of wrecking every aspect of my life. Jesus could probably do a better job of handling me than I could. In fact, the gardener could probably do a better job. It was either curl up under the covers and die of self-hatred, or, well, what the hell.

What I understood later was that the words in the pink shower that day were an invitation into a life of meaning.

I love being old enough to have an interesting past. After the pink-shower incident where I turned some sort of a corner, I ended up with even more failures—a divorce, a minimum wage job as a gift store clerk (with a master's degree), and continued rejections, sprinkled with publications in what seemed like the ratio of one to one hundred. Eventually, I married again, a handsome, brilliant, kind man with deep roots in Austin, and felt set for life—I had lived in twenty-one places at the ripe old age of twenty-seven, and would never have to move again. I loved my husband, and we settled in to have a normal, lovely life.

Four years later, my stable and secure husband quit the law practice and went to seminary, moving from Texas to Virginia. We ran through his law retirement fund before we got out.

We hit seven and a half years of infertility.

When my husband graduated, we lived at close to subsistence level for a number of years, starting over at the bottom.

Life in the church was a fishbowl, a near-disaster for a strong introvert like me.

We moved to four new towns over the next few years.

Among the eleven family members that we lost during one four-year period, three of them were murdered in their own home. We had to watch the reconstructed murder scene on television.

Then our children hit the teenage years and suffered most of the problems I had ever read about.

I quit my job at the university because the workplace was toxic.

I had a tumor the size of a big gumball at the base of my brain, removed through my nose.

My daughter had to be transported by helicopter to San Antonio in the middle of the night because she almost lost her second child.

Yeah.

Life from the outside didn't look like the Promised Land, in spite of the fact that I was a Christian.

The inside life, however, has left me with one truth over any other: God can redeem anything. The more bad things that happened, the more my life increased in meaning.

The human life span is lived in segments: childhood, teenage years, early adulthood, and so on. Each individual life has segments, too. I've heard people say, oh, that took place during the Chicago years. Or, that was a golden time, when the kids were in grade school. Or, that was when I worked for the telephone company before I moved to Dell.

Each juncture, each passage, requires a new search for meaning. Trailing spouses cry, what am I doing in this godforsaken city? The spouse with the job asks, why is this new situation so hard—did I make a mistake?

Each new circumstance is a fresh start, a new chapter in the book of meaning.

I can speak for no one but myself (and, in a way, I am writing this for myself as well as other people wondering about life, hoping faith is real). But because I am addicted to meaning, I will press on and walk through the fire to the other side, even if I don't get much sleep, or if my stomach knots.

Suffering has many guises—some suffering is like wearing a lead-lined coat. Other suffering is like swallowing a rose bush or living underwater without an oxygen tank or being buried alive. But no matter what shape the suffering takes, the process of getting through it is similar, sort of like drinking a nasty green smoothie that smells like the inside of a barn—something good for you, but miserable to swallow.

Suffering is a small death—death of hope, death of trust, death of health, death of happiness, death of expectation. Bereavement of the thing lost follows the traditional stages of grief. First, denial: "This awful thing didn't really happen—not now. Not to me!" followed by fury, usually at God, "Why? Why? Why are You letting this happen?" We turn our back on the Being we trusted to keep us safe from heartache.

Who wants to believe in a God that allows terrible things to happen to those He says He loves?

At this point, anger at God is almost a knee-jerk reaction. We confuse the promise of God's love with a promise to protect us from the barbs of the world. However, God's love does not mean walling us into a garden with no thorns on the rose bushes. Even in the garden of God's love, blizzards strike, plants wither, and we get pricked by all kinds of hardships.

The next step in the process in overcoming misery is deep and serious sulking, which can take thirty minutes or thirty years. It's good to limit the pity party, but not to repress it because it's an important stage in getting over life's wounds. Only after we eat all the poor-me cake and throw away the sagging streamers can we then allow hints of healing thoughts to waft in under the door.

The dialogue continues, going back and forth: maybe it wasn't God who inflicted the wound. Oh, yeah? Even if He didn't inflict the wound, He still let it happen. So it's still His fault. He doesn't love me after all. Well, maybe He does love me. Maybe He wants me to learn something important, something I wouldn't learn without suffering. Okay, okay, we say, maybe there's something He's trying to show me. But just for the record, I DON'T WANT TO LEARN IT.

Sometimes it takes weeks, sometimes years, and sometimes decades, but if we keep the conversation going, eventually a gift arrives.

Life inflicts pain. Period. No one who reaches adulthood avoids suffering, no matter what it looks like from the outside to other people. No matter what faith system we choose to trust. Nobody is exempt.

Walking home can be a dangerous proposition at night, but meaning is like the front porch light left on. We can't escape suffering, but we can keep an eye on the distant twinkle in the night. It's giving in to suffering that kills us—we either die literally, or we shrivel into a bitter form of nonbeing.

Meaning. Choice. Part of growing up is looking out for the gift that arrives following the pain. The new spouse after the love of your life walks out. The new career after you got ejected from your dream job. New friends after a troubled relocation. The feeling of new life after the doctor extracts the tumor.

When my children go through hard times, I tell them, "Watch. Keep a lookout to see how God will turn this ache into something good. Because He will. Sooner or later. After all, you kids were the redemption that came out of seven and a half years of despair."

There are two things wrong with ending the discussion of meaning at this point. The first issue goes back to the question of consensual reality. What is meaningful for me is not necessarily meaningful for everybody, and the way God redeems the suffering in any given person's life is unique to that person. The arrival of two children created the deepest meaning for me, but the arrival of children could be a nightmare for someone who does NOT want children.

Redemption looks different for different people. This phenomenon is especially true in families and can cause chaos instead of meaningful relationships for grown children. Parents raise children in the reality they construct. Children grow up and develop their own value systems, stocking their own shelves with what is meaningful to them—which is often a very different pantry from the parents' stash of values. When parents realize that their treasured delicacies have been thrown out by the children and replaced with a different taste all together, then family dinners are likely to be miserable instead of meaningful. (And vice versa if the children try to force their new views on entrenched parents. Parents tend to feel attacked if a child tries to suggest a new way to look at life.)

The search for meaning is an individual trip.

The second issue is that looking for meaning in what the world offers inevitably leads to disappointment. Not all suffering is redeemable in the world's terms. For instance, even though the two young men who murdered my aunt, uncle, and cousin were caught and punished, my relatives could not be brought back to life. Were their deaths just a senseless act of violence? Nobody wants to think that suffering is needless or without some glimmer of meaning.

Like happiness, meaning is an inside job. Take a billionaire whose chief purpose in life is to make money. Squeezing money out of every deal, spending money, hoarding money—his wealth makes him feel alive, worthwhile. This billionaire has attached money to his central core of worth. He defines himself by his money; he *is* his money.

Then he loses his money. Not only does he have to sell the big house, fancy car, and yacht, but he feels that life has lost its meaning. He is no one. If he can't either finagle a way to make more money, come to terms with what has happened, or realize that he is more than his money, then he is stuck in despair and nihilism.

Life's debacles tender meaning if we choose to look. Perhaps a larger gift is at stake for the former billionaire. Though money gave him satisfaction, it didn't give him joy. With the right attitude and the grace of God, this billionaire is now in the position to learn one of the world's greatest truths: money doesn't make you happy.

One reason Christianity is an attractive option for me is that God's gift basket overflows, even as the world rains oobleck or worse on us. At its best, the world gives satisfaction, and satisfaction in the extreme is satedness, an unpleasant state, like needing to throw up after eating too many pancakes dripping with butter and syrup. On the other hand, what God gives is fulfillment, whose extreme state is joy.

Big difference. Knowing the limits of what the world can give is essential in the search for meaning. Sooner or later, the world will disappoint.

For me, the only thing that has fulfilled the deepest angst, the deepest suffering is the grace of God. In one sense, my journey so far is figuring out that the gifts of the world are truly delicious and give immediate pleasure—but they don't last and the hunger returns.

What suffering has taught me—and life isn't over, so I'll probably have to learn this lesson again—is that underneath all the pain and all the longing and the attempts to fill the inner hole with meaning is a search for love. To be loved down to my shoelaces, in spite of myself. For a kid who grew up in a strict household dominated by alcoholism—where love was parceled out like pennies according to how nice we were—being loved no matter what was a new thing. I grew up a crippled bird, and this new *unconditional* love that Jesus offers feels like soaring.

Deep meaning, for me, comes from outside anything the world can offer. My experience has shown time and again—because, yes, I've needed the lesson over and over—that the love of God is the meaning of life.

3

THE ARMCHAIR GRANDFATHER

God has been replaced by karma,
luck, good fortune, fate,
and Mother Nature.
—Source unknown

MY GRANDFATHER, DONDI, WAS A dentist in Durant, Oklahoma, and had a small private museum of artifacts in the lobby of his office. At home, he always sat in a gray nubby armchair, reading the newspaper. When he got to the comics, he let me pile in his lap as he read them out loud. Dondi took miles and miles of moving pictures of my sisters and me performing our latest tricks—wobbling on skates, dressed up in our aunts' old ball gowns, making mud pies with cherries on the top. He bought me a ukulele; he sat me down on the enormous porch swing and told me that the world was my oyster, but it was my job to find the pearls.

Dondi died when I was thirteen, and I lost the only person who had expressed unconditional love, who had loved me just because I existed. After that, I spent much of my life searching for Dondi in everyone else I met.

I learned in seminary that God was bigger than any words or images we could come up with for Him. The limitation of our brains, however, has never stopped anybody from trying, and these efforts are categorized by two Greek words I've had to look up just now because I can't remember them. *Cataphatic* means descriptions of what God is, and *apophatic* means everything God isn't. Example: God is good; God isn't evil.

Though I was stuffed chock full of God talk and Bible stories from the time I escaped the church nursery at three and moved into big girl Sunday school, God remained a distant concept, sort of like the idea of mountains to a girl from Oklahoma. Mountains didn't become real until I went to Colorado and saw the Front Range for myself.

Another example would be my uncle, who was a vice-president of General Dynamics in New York. The company he worked for might as well have been the moon as far as I was concerned, (only I could see the moon, and General Dynamics remained some vague notion of a complicated, important Thing housed in a skyscraper far, far away).

My uncle himself, on the other hand was a huge man with black curly hair, a broad face, and a laugh like a sonic boom that burst the sound barrier, shaking the silverware on the table. As a representation of his company, my uncle was real, but General Dynamics was not. Perhaps if I had visited his office and seen maps, I would have had a clearer idea.

Jean Piaget, Swiss developmental psychologist and philosopher, pegged the "Formal Operational" developmental stage at early adolescence, when children can begin to comprehend abstractions. Some children can feel the presence of God at a young age, like I knew when my uncle was in the room. One of my friends experienced the presence of God at five years old and insisted her parents take her to church. What a spiritual gift—five years old and God was already real to her.

Not me. I could talk about God, but He didn't become real until I was twelve. He came one Easter weekend as I was helping the Altar Guild polish brass plates on the pews, and then He left again after the Sunday service.

Still, by twelve, I'd caught a spiritual glimpse of the reason for all the fuss on Sunday mornings. For a brief weekend, I experienced the great power Who had created the universe and me, the One who is in charge of everything beyond my understanding.

It was just a peek, but it was enough. I felt loved and warm, and I've never forgotten that Easter. Even though the girl sitting next to me sang a flat alto, grating on my ears, I felt in my bones the presence of God.

If I'm going to take this faith reevaluation seriously, I need to go back to the beginning of religion. Any religion—those early, fascinating quests for God. A brief history of world-wide religion goes like this:

Stage One: "Gods Behaving Badly." Early Greeks, Romans, Assyrians, Egyptians, Norwegians, Germans, among others, created a cast of larger-than-life characters who fought like cats and dogs, made selfish demands, did dreadful things to each other and to the poor human beings who crossed them. The abduction and rape of Persephone, for instance, ranks right up there with the top ten soaps on daytime television.

These early gods should have known better. The former citizens of Mount Olympus have been demoted these days from gods to myths. Though their escapades still provide entertainment, their antics and relationships no longer explain the universe.

Stage Two: "One God, Head Boss." A monotheistic god—not a mountain filled with incestuous, vengeful super heroes. This God created us in His image and not vice versa. The granddaddy of all Jews, Christians, and Muslims, Abraham fathered three religions under this one God.

Stage Three, the current stage: "A Smorgasbord of Belief." A religious buffet with more choices than Golden Corral. Hinduism, Buddhism, Shintoism, Taoism, Deism, Materialism, and on and on down the line until Atheism.

The study of world religions tells us three things about ourselves as creatures inhabiting this global village: (1) we seek an explanation of why the world works as it does, (2) we crave inner peace, and (3) we hunger for pure goodness in a being higher than our petty selves.

Except the atheists, who don't seem to care. Life on the rock is all there is. And, of course, the materialists, who prefer to go shopping and not worry about these mysteries.

Waking up in the morning involves going through the turnstile between a dream world amusement park of fantasy and terror and the roads and byways of our waking, rational decisions. Who is God, as we climb in the vehicles of our lives and drive down the interstate of daily life? Is God a roadside service station? Is God a passenger? Belief in a vague, kind, benevolent higher power is the easiest religious route—a Being who gives us what we pray for, who stays out of our nitty gritty personal business, and who loves us no matter what we do. We can stay on cruise control until we hit a disaster.

"God is great; God is good. Let us thank Him for our food." Having repeated this grace before meals approximately 17,520 times before leaving for college, I understood the importance of thanking God (although in the subsystem of our family, I knew it was Dad who paid for the food and Mom who cooked it). Still, I knew gratitude was the proper response for not being one of the starving Chinese children my parents referred to when I didn't want to eat Brussels sprouts.

"Great" and "good," though, baffled a child's mind. Oklahoma University's football team in the Bud Wilkinson era was a "great" team. Elizabeth Taylor was a "great" actress. The United States of America was a "great" country. Somehow, God was greater than all of these.

"Good" was even harder to grasp. In the apophatic sense, I knew what was not good. My classmate who stole all the students' erasers and hid them in her cigar box was not good. Refusing to share with my sister the vanilla ice cream cone I got from Dairy Queen was not good. Hiding out from Sunday school in the bathroom with two of my friends was not good.

How on earth could anyone or anything be pure good all the time? Certainly not I.

Over the course of my life, I've known lots of good people, friends who let you pick the movie, who notice when something is bothering

you, who give to charity, and whose amiable personalities make them fun to be with. These good people don't take themselves too seriously and are determined to leave the world a better place than they found it.

Another type of good people are those who are downright saccharine. They look on the bright side, yes, but with relentless, blinding, and devastating good cheer. They compete for self-sacrifice. This kind of goodness is cloying; these good people are no fun.

Earthly goodness can become boring after awhile. If only Miss Goody Two-shoes would say a bad word even once, just to prove that she's not perfect in her own eyes. Consciousness of one's own goodness is called self-righteousness, and it smells to high heaven, like the tomb of a dead person.

If God is pure goodness, then there's good news and bad news and more good news. The first good news is that the creator force made us good, in His image. We are good! We were created good! This God-given goodness wraps around us like the electric warming suits worn by pilots in World War II, enabling them to keep toasty in subzero temperatures. True goodness is God's embrace. Forever.

The bad news is that we blow the fuse in our electric suits. Adam and Eve started it. We steal. We lie. We drink too much. We gossip. We insist on our way or the highway, regardless. We wake up in the morning on the wrong side of the bed, and we spread our crummy mood around like moldy jam on bread. If we tell ourselves we don't do any of the above, then, woops! We've slid into self-righteousness, and we all know what that smells like.

The beginning of redemption for me was realizing in a pink shower stall that anything (actually, almost everything at that time in my life) I did was tinged with non-good. When he examined himself for the first time, C.S. Lewis said, "And there I found what appalled me; a zoo of lusts, a bedlam of ambitions, a nursery of fears, a harem of fondled hatreds. My name was legion."

What a miserable self-insight. Aren't donors who do enormous good to worthy charities—aren't they allowed just a teeny bit of pleasure in seeing their names in the list of contributors to the cause? Or, as I heard once in a sermon, there's the little bit of envy in every congratulations—isn't it better to offer the congratulations in spite of the envy rather than sniffing away in a huff? Or letting friends know the depth of sacrifice we've made for their well-being, because we love them so much (and because we want them to know what good, good people we are)?

I am hopeless. I just hate to admit it.

Most of us leave a bread crumb trail of self-interest on a lifelong path of doing good. We can't help it. Human effort, even when aimed at the good of others, leaves trace evidence of ourselves and our neediness in even the most worthy acts.

The other good news, though, after the bad news, is that God's goodness is pure. God is the solid chocolate bunny, while we are the hollow ones. Which means that sometimes, if we pray and mean it, He increases our goodness. Our real goodness, our warm goodness.

The other good news about God's goodness is that His goodness never turns sappy and boring. It always feels, well, good.

God as parent emerged early as a characteristic of the creator force. Parents create babies, so the relationship makes sense. However, not everyone had Ward Cleaver as a father, so thinking of God as Father can be problematic if one's father was a hurtful person. The last thing anybody wants is a God who seems abusive, or doesn't care, or doesn't have our best interests in mind.

Parenting, as it turns out, is a daunting endeavor. The cute, soft bundles of joy quickly assert themselves as their own, independent little persons. We cannot fluff them and prop them up on the bed like our favorite stuffed animals and resume our lives for the day. No, they cry. They defy us from the moment their little rosebud lips can form the word *no*.

My father had many good qualities. He took the time to show me how to throw a baseball and to play tennis. He provided well for all of us, and he had a great sense of humor. But he was a self-admitted alcoholic, which brought with it a deep sense of shame and unworthiness. Even though he was later active in the Twelve-Steps movement, he passed on to his children a low self-esteem. I entered adulthood with all the personal self-confidence of pond scum.

Thinking of God as father did not bring comfort during dark times. Until one day, I heard the Lord's Prayer. Differently. The Lord's Prayer starts out "Our Father, who art in heaven." What I heard was I had *another* father, besides the father who wore baggy pajamas and slept it off in the next room.

And this father was a different kind of guy. This father knew how to parent. God was parent I could trust and emulate as a parent to my own children.

Fifteen minutes before supper, my kids used to stand in the kitchen, begging for candy from the snack basket on top of the refrigerator. "No," I told them. "Supper's almost ready and you'll spoil your appetite."

They wailed, "You don't love me!"

Good parenting does not mean giving children whatever they want, when they want it. God knows this. For years, I kept a card posted on the wall near my desk: "Faith is knowing that God has your best interests in mind when He answers no to your prayers."

A good parent, like God, knows that actions have consequences (goodness gracious, I sound just like my mother), but it's true. My son came home upset because a boy at school had hit him. "I'm so sorry, honey. What happened right before he hit you?" I asked.

"I called him a big fat pig."

"Oh. I see. Do you think that what you said had anything to do with the fact that he hit you?"

"But he is a big fat pig."

"Yes, but by telling him, you hurt his feelings. No wonder he hit you."

"You're taking his side!" Then, "You don't love me!"

I had to become a parent myself to understand that God was not distant, cruel, or uncaring when He allowed me to suffer the consequences for actions or choices I had made. Just because God doesn't wear a cardigan doesn't mean that He isn't the father who knows best.

Sometimes it takes decades to look back and see what God's purpose was in denying us what we thought we'd die for if we didn't get. Oh, we say. Now I get it. He had our best interests in mind all along.

Here are some examples of bad things (usually happening in clumps, of course) that are easy to blame on God as a bad parent. Not only does Aunt Matilda die, but right after she dies, the dog runs away, we trip and sprain an ankle, and the house burns down.

God parents us in all three tenses, past, present, and future.

If God is a loving parent, then how can He allow these bad things to happen?

The bitterness and despair of tragedy keeps many people from breaking through the wall in the wilderness into the secret garden of faith just beyond. I used to stand clawing at the rough bricks of the wall from the outside, shivering, when a few steps around the corner a wooden door stood cracked open, ready for me to enter.

God parents us in all three tenses, past, present, and future. God created the world good, a place where nothing bad ever happened, where the inhabitants had enough to eat, where no one killed each other, where no one died, and where bodies were free of disease. Paradise was the original plan.

Then, well, things got MUBAR (messed up beyond all recognition). Adam and Eve ate the fruit. That incident started the chain reaction of pain in childbirth, back-breaking work, envying your brother and killing him, and all the other awful stuff that life on earth brings. What's worse is that we continue to eat the fruit. The transition from paradise to hell on earth happens daily when we forget that God is the parent and we are not in charge of the planet.

Just like any other parent, God can sometimes step in and intervene to prevent a Terrible Thing from happening. Just last week from across the river, my son saw a child drowning. He called out to my grandson, aged eight, who jumped in, lifted the child out of the depths and brought him to shore where he was revived.

Also like any good parent, God knows that we learn from our mistakes and the mistakes of others. He stands ready to comfort us when we fall. When my baby sister tripped on the new rug and cut her head open, my mother scooped her up, cuddled her, and rushed her to the hospital. Through the pain, my sister basked in the love of my mother. It did no good to blame Mother for buying the rug that my sister tripped on.

Blaming God for allowing tragedies is a destructive approach to handling pain. God created paradise for us, but in this life now, stuff happens in a warped and imperfect world. God is the loving parent who stands with His arms open, ready to cuddle us when our heads get bashed. Why God allows suffering—a subject as big as a black hole, but like the definition of a black hole—is anything but empty space; in fact, it's where we get pulled gravitationally into finding clues in the densely packed matter of God's existence. Exploration of this scary phenomenon is a solo journey, like Sandra Bullock floating in space with a thin life cord, but essential in accepting the benevolence of a Higher Power. At least it has been for me.

Omniscience is a scary word. When I was five, my father's mother died. She was also my godmother and had given me a beautiful white leather prayer book. In explaining that Grandmommy was now in heaven, my father somehow implied that she and God were up in the sky, looking into my life as if my brain were a dollhouse, and they could see every single thought, motive, and desire of my heart.

No, thank you.

Grandmommy must have lost interest in the secrets of a five-year-old because I lost the sense of her voyeurism in my life. But what about God? Did He know I stuck my tongue out at Susie behind her back? That I sneaked candy? Did He care? What was He going to do to me if He found out?

Omnipotent is another scary word, and put together with *omniscient*, it meant I didn't stand a chance. If God knew everything about me and could do anything He wanted, then I'd better watch out for lightning and for the wolves I just knew were hiding behind the trees in our backyard.

The questions grew even greater as I emerged out of the wolf-terror stage. Again, if God can do anything, why doesn't He prevent hurricanes and train wrecks? If God already knows everything in advance, why do we need confession? What is the point of making decisions?

The answers I discovered as I tripped, stumbled, and roiled through the next decades, weren't answers. Job, covered with open sores sitting on the ash heap, his children dead, his fortunes ruined—alone in the world except for a bitter wife and three idiot friends—discovered that the love of God and His presence trumps everything.

What happens to us on earth, good and bad, is a means to an end—a relationship with the divine. The father or mother's name on a birth certificate is no guarantee that the man who sired the child or the woman who bore her will be around to care for the child. However, God's name is written on our spiritual birth certificates, and as parent, He desires very much to be around to care for us, to comfort us, to listen to us, to relate to us.

The creator force could have left the planet with rocks, plants, and simple life forms. But He didn't. He created human beings to shower His love on. This is the key to the garden.

The English word *love* ought to wear a sign around its neck warning people not to use it carelessly. The same word is used for how we feel about dark chocolate and our soul mate. "Love" can mean, "I only want to have sex with you," or "I want to walk with you through your ordeal with cancer." We love Pekinese dogs, we love pickleball, we love the new outfit we got on sale; we also love our spouse, our children, our best friends, our hometown.

There is no such thing as bad love, in spite of country-western songs. If God is love and God is good, then all love is good. However, in the boot camp for eternity that we call life on earth—the rigorous preparation for the rest of our lives—earthly love often gets off-center, cattywampus, crooked.

To say, "the essence of God is love" is to invite as many interpretations of love as there are people. Simple example: a woman needs her husband to listen and hold her when she's upset. The husband thinks he's showing love by interrupting her to fix her problem. Love is present, but misperceived.

To some, love means never having to say you're sorry. For others, never apologizing is a bunch of hooey—asking and receiving forgiveness is the grease that keeps the relationship going.

If we have this much trouble navigating love with each other, how can we possibly understand the love of God?

Literature is riddled with love gone wrong. Fairy tales often end with "happily ever after," but not until the heroes have faced dragons, wicked witches, cruel stepmothers, poisonous apples, and other threats to well-being. Fairy tales may end well, but they are terrifying. I read years ago that when Disney's *Snow White* came out, theaters had to reupholster all the seats because tiny children lost bladder control when the witch appeared.

Grown-up literature contains terrors, too, and no guarantees the story will end well. Life itself is even more ambiguous, and daily, it seems, we have to clean up the messes of "love gone wrong."

If God is love, pure and good, then what in the heck is the matter down here on earth? Love—always good in itself—is warped and mangled by human beings. Dante saw three problems with misused love: (1) too much love, (2) not enough love, and (3) love/desire for the wrong object.

Novels, television, and the movies have made a killing on too much love. *Fatal Attraction,* for example, starts out with powerful love (though leaning toward the side of lust) between a man and a woman he meets, but when the man returns to his wife, the woman stalks him, tries to murder him because she can't let go of the love she feels. Love has become obsession.

Then there's the famous Norman Bates, whose mother created a monster out of her son by smothering him with too much love.

Human relationships become tar pits due to overzealous love, entrapping us in a black gooey emotional mess. But excess love for people is only part of the problem. What about our excess love for things?

Too much love for money leads to greed. Too much love for control leads to tyranny. Too much love for self leads to narcissism and vanity. Too much love for food leads to gluttony. Too much love for accomplishment leads to pride. And around and around we go on the carousel of excess desire.

Enough, as it turns out, is as good as a feast. Enough money leads to happiness. Enough food leads to health. Enough self-love leads to confidence. Enough accomplishments lead to a good reputation. Enough control leads to a good balance in life.

The trouble begins when we love too much.

On the other side of the stadium of life sit those who love too little. Children translate attention as love, and we all know the story of Johnny who acts out at school because he is neglected at home. Any attention is better than none. Starving for love leads to prostitution, clingy relationships, needy children, and a deep sense of worthlessness.

Due to each person's particular recipe of DNA blended with experience and upbringing, we vary in our capability to love and receive love. Some people have the capacity of a walnut shell to contain love; others can contain—and give out in return—a vat of love, overflowing onto the people around them. Whatever our capacity to accept, hold, and exchange this most precious commodity, we all desire to be filled to the brim. We are beggars for love, our hands outstretched, clasping a cup, hoping for contributions from passersby.

We give each other what we can. But we can give only what we've been given, and the world is filled with people who've been shorted by love, for whom love has been doled out, squeezed into their cups drop by miserable drop, and given at such a price that they measure love in microscopic molecules.

Only when God walks by is the cup filled to overflowing.

The third problem with love on the earth is love for the wrong object, a target that creates a distorted trajectory, mayhem, and the rest of the big no-no's. A politician, for example, loves to win more than he or she loves integrity, thus stuffing the ballot box, getting indicted. A woman lusts after another woman's husband, divorces her own husband, ends up alone when the object of her love decides to stay with his wife after all. A man wants what the other brother has, kills the brother, and wanders the earth forever with a mark on his forehead.

"Looking for love in all the wrong places" could be a theme song for our culture, right up there with the national anthem. We are a people convinced that love can be gotten, earned, bought, and sold. When a woman I know was three, she and her parents lived in rural Texas. When she and her mother went into the city to the grocery store, my friend insisted that her mother buy Kool-Aid. As soon as they arrived home, the little girl urged her mother to hurry up with the Kool-Aid, and as the mother stirred the pitcher, my friend anxiously skittered around the kitchen, looking under the table and in the corners. Finally, when her mother poured her a glass, she cried in despair, "Where are the friends?"

She had seen an ad for Kool-Aid on television. As soon as the TV mother poured the powder into a pitcher of water, all sorts of cartoon characters and real children appeared in the kitchen to play with the little girl.

Adults know better, sort of. The fact remains that advertising works on a subliminal level. Between the lines, the luxury car ad promises that you will catch the beloved or increase your popularity or boost your self-esteem. It's not just any set of wheels.

What America doesn't advertise is the gap between the ability to purchase the car—and the love, friendship, or respect the car fails to produce.

God's love bypasses the car, the girl, the money. God stands in front of the TV right in our living room, offering the real thing for free. The gap occurs only if we sit in the recliner and say, "No thank you."

I love America, but our movies and television package false promises, like the Christmas presents wrapped under a large decorative tree in the mall—colorful, bright, and inviting, but covering nothing but empty cardboard boxes.

And so we scavenge for love, affection, friendship the best we can, but this scavenger hunt is a hit-or-miss proposition. If we ignore or can't see the gift of love standing right in our living room, often we start ringing doorbells in our never-ending search for the kind of love we think will fill us up.

Love from a mate, a spouse, a lover, a one-night stand; love from friends, children, families. We keep ringing the doorbells—and too often insensitive people, narcissists, perverts, abusers answer the door. Or people too busy to care.

Love from a father, approval, attention that we never got. We go from house to house, looking for what we never had, each doorbell answered, often with disappointment.

We continue ringing doorbells until we find what we're looking for. Or not. Sometimes we ring doorbells for life, when the answer is standing right in front of us.

My grandfather, Dondi, showed me an inkling of the rare and twinkling phenomenon of unconditional love. I have no doubt that he would have disciplined me if I'd done something terrible—that's part of love, after all. But no matter what, Dondi made me feel lovable. Even when I was silly, needed attention, pouted, argued with my sisters, Dondi let me climb in his lap in the gray nubby armchair.

Like the birth father who contributed to our physical creation—the set of stubby toes we inherited, our curly hair, brown eyes, and the tendency to walk fast—God the Father created us good and loves us to death. Literally. Loves us past death on earth, and loves us so much He came to earth and died for us.

God loves each of us as if we were His only child.

Living east of Eden, we live in an imperfect and painful world, and we get caught with our hands in the cookie jar of life, guilty as sin with crumbs all over our faces. God the father doesn't beat us for our transgressions, doesn't withhold love, doesn't imply that He'll love us only if we're good, doesn't abuse us to make Himself feel better. Because God made us and knows us to the core, He lets us crawl in His lap for comfort.

For me, this love is an important part of the Christian faith—too important to disregard.

4

Been There, Done That, Got the T-shirt

All great truths begin as blasphemies.
—George Bernard Shaw from
Annajanska the Bolshevik Empress

ONE PARTICULAR CHRISTMAS, I bought 130 gifts, hand-selected, hand-wrapped, and hand-delivered—presents for children, parents, aunts, uncles, cousins, neighbors, friends, godchildren, vestry, staff, and teachers. That year in Houston, Christmas No. 1 occurred early Christmas morning, when two excited children woke us up shortly after dawn. When it was all over (around seven o'clock that morning), we ate casserole and monkey bread with my mother, who was visiting.

Christmas No. 2 that same year occurred a day later, when we arrived at my father's house in Austin, with another round of presents that he and my stepmother had wrapped in newspaper comics—and afterward we ate a lunch of his special black bean soup. Christmas No. 3 occurred that afternoon when we crossed town for yet another tree load of gifts, followed by turkey, ham, sweet potatoes, and three kinds of pie (with ice cream) at my in-laws.

Two days later, worn out from over-celebrating, as well as sick, exhausted, coughing, and aching all over, we drove back to Houston and the four of us walked into the doctor's office before we even made it home. Fortunately, no one had thrown up in the car.

Each year for over a decade, we struggled through multiple Christmases with scattered family members, and every year on New Year's, I resolved (threatened) to leave for the south of France, *all by myself*, the next December. For a month. Beneath the crumpled mounds of tissue paper, the abandoned lists of things to do, and late Christmas cards, I had lost the baby Jesus.

Two years ago, my father and my mother-in-law died a month apart. Christmas changed. Everything changed. I needed to find the baby Jesus again.

After my father's death, I began to reexamine the planks, nails, and design of the house of faith I'd been living in, making sure that the Christian religion is the address I want to keep until I die. But questions drum like rain on the roof: Why is God three parts—the Father and the Son and the Holy Spirit—instead of God alone?

Who is Jesus Christ? And why is He so important?

My father went to seminary when I was a baby, only to turn around and return to the oil business, not the priesthood. A year or so later, he had a religious conversion experience by the side of the road. From that point on, it was Jesus this and Jesus that, always talking about this invisible man who lived at church and who was too good to be true. My father wanted me to give my life to Jesus. He wanted it very much.

Though I was not a spiritually gifted little girl, around age nine I gave in to my dad's pleas, which he often cranked up at bedtime prayers. I ran after him one night and caught him while he was standing at the liquor cabinet getting ready to mix drinks. The irony of making a religious commitment right there at the liquor cabinet with an alcoholic father about to start tippling is inescapable, but I'm not making this stuff up. He said a prayer with me. After he finished, I wanted to feel saintly, to say my life changed. But it didn't, so I went back to bed.

Dad followed up my "conversion" with a blizzard of pamphlets, material geared for children to learn to pray properly. He also gave me a white leather Bible that matched my prayer book—information about God that was supposed to make me understand Him better. Frankly, God was too vague for me to be interested in, and I cared more about having sleepovers with my friends (we called them slumber parties, although very little slumber took place) and writing book reports at school.

My faith—such as it was—fell asleep for many years, except for that one glimmer at Easter time when I was twelve.

About the time of my so-called conversion at age nine, I stared up at the picture of Jesus in the Episcopal Church Sunday school class, a three-quarter profile of a man with long golden brown locks and a misty yellow aura around a WASP face. The teacher said that Jesus was my friend.

I didn't have any friends who looked like that.

My parents didn't have any friends who looked like that either, certainly not the men in the 1950s, sporting crew cuts and suits with skinny ties.

We moved from Oklahoma to Indiana when I was ten, and the Quaker Sunday school classroom had the same picture of Jesus, looking up at the sky.

So this Jesus was everywhere, everybody's friend—but not the run-of-mill kind of buddy who played jump rope at school or came over to the house for cocktails with my parents. No, He lived at church, and His closest friends gathered there on Sundays to look at His picture, to sing songs to Him, and to discuss in lengthy sentences what was bothering them.

Apparently, Jesus had been a real person once, living long ago in a place far away where they had camels and no hospitals to be born in. Not like the Tooth Fairy, but a historical figure, and this I could understand. We'd studied George Washington, Queen Elizabeth, and Rachel Jackson, and all of them had lived a long time ago. Like Jesus.

When someone near and dear to me recently announced, "Jesus never lived. It's all an Internet hoax," I did a Google search for the historical Jesus. All the past reliable sources were intact: Pliny, Tacitus, Josephus— references to Jesus Christ *outside the Bible*. Oh, He was real, okay.

That wasn't the problem. The problem was that Jesus was a troublemaker. He was a convicted criminal, and who can believe that a convicted criminal was the Son of God? It's easier to deny that He ever existed.

But He did exist. He riled up the people, threatened the religious establishment, and turned the Jewish faith upside down. The religious and political authorities finally had enough of this rabble-rouser and killed Him.

The trouble with the life of Jesus, besides the ruckus He caused, is the rumor of His resurrection three days after He died.

Unable to shake a scholar's writing habits completely, I can't resist including three resources to give some oomph to the argument. Skip them if you like. Tacitus, Roman senator and historian, reports on Nero's decision to blame Rome's famous fire in 64 CE on the Christians, mentioning Christ, His death under Pontius Pilate, and the "mischievous superstition" that broke out after His death, spreading from Judea to Rome.

Pliny the Younger, an imperial magistrate, writes to the Emperor Trajan about how to carry out the Roman law against the Christians. He was happy to torture or execute these illegal religious people, but there were so many of them, of every age, social class, and gender. They were treating Christ as a god!

Josephus, a Roman Jewish scholar and historian mentions Jesus in "Testimonium Flavianum": "About this time there lived Jesus, a wise man... [who] wrought surprising feats... He was the Christ...." Josephus goes on to tell of Jesus' crucifixion under Pontius Pilate and His resurrection on the third day, a belief that had not disappeared among the Christian "tribe."

Trusting historical sources as well as anyone can trust historical sources (which is not a given), we know that Jesus was a man who walked the earth like the rest of us—in Judea. Jesus Christ is not a myth, the way some of the ancient gods are.

Here is His vita:

1. Born in Bethlehem; traveled to Egypt; returned to Judea
2. Grew up in Hicksville, the town of Nazareth, where He was a carpenter until age 30
3. Itinerant preacher for three years
4. Teacher, moralist, ethicist, theologian
5. Healer of blindness, leprosy, demon possession, and other illnesses
6. Popular rabbi around Galilee, hoofing it from city to city
7. Charismatic speaker endorsing love, joy, and peace
8. Agitator among the people, promoting a new religion based on the Old Testament
9. Crucified criminal
10. Teachings still available at your local bookstore and on Amazon.com

This encapsulated version of the historical Jesus doesn't deal with the problem; back then, teachers like Jesus were a dime a dozen. But the Resurrection business. That was a problem. After He'd been dead three days, people saw Him wandering around the garden Sunday morning. Then, He hung around for forty days visiting friends, finally ascending into heaven in front of a crowd, a spectacle much like a huge helicopter rescue operation.

Here is the rub. Is this story one massive forty-day hallucination? Did Jesus really die on the cross, or was He just tortured until He passed out? Did His followers use tricks with smoke and mirrors to prove Jesus was the Messiah?

The problem for the Roman government was that the rumor didn't die out. It spread like a grassfire in dry August heat, flaming through the entire Roman Empire.

Since people are still arguing over these same questions two thousand years later, I suspect that Something happened three days after the Roman soldiers locked Jesus in the tomb and rolled a boulder over the entrance.

Otherwise, what was the hubbub about? What's the point?

I have kept up with a precious handful of childhood and college friends, e-mailing and meeting yearly in B & B's, spas, hotel rooms in cities all over—anyplace we can get together. Over the years, our friendships continue to blossom. You'd think we'd run out of things to say after fifty-plus years, but the opposite is true. We talk each other's ears off when we get together.

Yes, Jesus is the friend from childhood, whom I barely knew in younger years, but with whom I have grown up. He is also my teacher. But He is also something more, because of the special thing that happened three days after He died.

I don't have trouble with the Resurrection—either Jesus' or ours because I heard a talk once at a conference that could have been called "Physics for Dummies," using scientific terms that even I could understand. Thanks to that lecture and Wikipedia, I now know what Einstein's famous equation means: $E=MC^2$. "E" stands for energy; "M" stands for mass, which is not quite the same thing as matter, but is more like the fundamental property of a body. "C" stands for *celeritas,* which is the speed of light.

Huddling in our den in Oklahoma when I was a child, our family watched a ferocious electrical storm—a sound and light show against the night as lightning threatened to take out all the city's power. The thunder was so loud it scared the stuffing out of us three kids. Our parents patted us and taught us to tell how far away the lightning was (to reassure us, I suppose, that our house wouldn't be attacked and burned by the jagged yellow, crooked bolts of electricity). "One Mississippi, two Mississippi, three Mississippi, four Mississippi, five Mississippi—and goodness gracious, see? The lightning is far away."

Given the facts about sound and light travel, Einstein figured out that energy is mass times the speed of light squared. Neither mass nor energy can be created or destroyed, but can only move from one location to another. Like reaching out to shake someone's hand and getting shocked. That's energy transfer on a personal level.

So what does this have to do with theology? This law of physics makes the claim that the mass of our being, as observed through the behavior, expressions, and gestures of the matter of our individual bodies, does not rot as does the matter, but the mass is converted into a different kind of energy at death.

Heaven, then, is a congregating place for all the mass of Being—our "souls" if you will—to gather after the matter of our bodies has been laid to rest.

Makes sense to me. As good as any other explanation anyway.

Jesus' resurrection was the prototype for our own resurrection. This good news has become better and better the older I get. Eternity doesn't register to a young person, but to someone my age, when the ultimate countdown—though still undetermined—has begun, eternity is a long time to be dead.

Stockton and I have been married for thirty-six years, and over that span, we've had several marriages—the swooning marriage, the practical marriage, the I-never-get-to-spend-time-with-you marriage, the comfortable marriage, the irritable marriage, and the retirement marriage, yet to come.

I've had several different lives, as well (we all do)—the whoopie life of excitement, the serious life, the working life, the sharing life, the spiritual life, the family life, the life with friends. However, at this stage, I've discovered there's only one life in which it makes a difference between whether we live for eternity or whether things just end, flat, kapooie—and that is the spiritual life, the life of prayer. This conversation is the one that doesn't end.

And when we want to discuss things with a supreme being who understands the human condition from the inside out, Jesus is the person to talk to.

In 1997, our church took a trip to the Holy Land, where, honest to goodness, the first thing off the bus, a young Arab lad offered to buy the associate minister's wife for a rather large number of goats and camels. She turned as purply red as an eggplant and her husband politely declined. After that memorable beginning in Jerusalem, we saw all the usual sights, the cave where Jesus was born, the upper room, the garden of Gethsemane, where some of the same trees were still living, gnarled and viney.

Sweat-drenched and guzzling water from a bottle, I remember staring at one particular stone in a rugged stairway along a route Jesus had walked. A rock that had been there for millennia. My Nikes and Jesus' sandals—along with millions of other shoes—had quite possibly touched the same stone.

The famous atheist, Sam Harris, speaks of walking in Jesus' footsteps, too, around the Sea of Galilee. "As I gazed at the surrounding hills, a feeling of peace came over me. It soon grew to a blissful stillness that silenced my thoughts. In an instant, the sense of being a separate self—an 'I' or a 'me'—vanished." He continues to explain that this feeling of transcendence can also be had in the dentist's chair, or at his desk. The issue is interpretation.

Yes, the equipment for experiencing spiritual epiphanies comes with the arms, legs, and minds of the human organism. And, yes, it can be a question of interpretation. Was it an inkling of the divine? Was it a crossed wire in the brain? Was it the lifting of a migraine with medication? Whatever it was, it was a gift, a pleasure, a deeply satisfying experience, and one that we cannot conjure at will.

No matter what we make of this ability to feel ourselves lifted out of ourselves, I'm grateful. Rather than thinking, "Yeah, yeah, yeah, it's nothing but an aspirin kicking in," it's more titillating to see these spiritual epiphanies as God's way of offering us tidbits from a future feast; besides, what other God has bothered to come to earth to help get us out of the messes we keep making for ourselves?

Centaurs, mermaids, fauns, wolf-man and the Sphinx—all these mythical creatures are hybrids, part human, part beast. Their outward form reflects their dual nature.

It took the early church three or four hundred years to figure out the dual nature of Christ, so I don't feel so bad that the issue is still confusing to me. On the outside, Jesus Christ looked like an ordinary man of His time. When He walked around Judea and Galilee, He did not have an aura attached to His head like a halo so people could recognize that He was divine as well as human, and this fact made it more difficult to determine just what this one-of-a-kind person was like.

Jesus' dual nature really threw early theologians for a loop. Some thought He was like a suitcase—ordinary on the outside, but carrying nuggets of divine gold on the inside. Others thought that He was human through and through, but inspired by God, like the rest of us, only more so. Still others figured He was a spiritual creature disguised as a human being.

Jesus Christ is an anomaly.

The human tendency is to dismiss what we can't explain. Two

thousand years later, we are still confounded by this irregular abnormality. As C. S. Lewis said, Jesus was either mentally ill, a liar, or who He said He was. We can choose to believe or not, or we can ignore the whole thing, which is probably easier in the short term.

And yet. Jesus is the dog that won't let go of the world's pants leg.

He keeps surfacing in odd places—the White House prayer breakfast, graffiti on the subway, the Internet. Sooner or later, it's best to deal with Him.

The origin of a cliché is often much more interesting than the cliché. For example, "it doesn't make an iota of difference." Picture a large international assembly at Nicea, with men in long robes arguing over whether Jesus was made of the same essence as God or whether He was merely a walking replica. Was Jesus the real deal or not?

At one end of the hall Arius holds forth, crying, "All those for homoousia raise your hand! Jesus is NOT made of the same substance as God!"

Hugging the microphone at the other end of the forum, Athenasius rallies his supporters on the opposing side, "Homoiousia! Homoiousia! Let's hear it for Jesus as God!"

Throughout the banquet as the bishops, archbishops, and other bigwigs in the early church had been served (no doubt) their roasted chicken and green beans, the followers of Arius and those of Athenasius hashed it out before the final vote. The only difference between "same substance" and "similar substance" was an "i," a Greek iota.

In this case the iota made all the difference. Jesus has the same DNA as God.

The question now arises, why did God see the need to come to earth in person, after living in the Holy of Holies in the Jewish temple for millennia?

In the movie *Honey, I Shrunk the Kids,* the kind but careless scientist accidentally shrinks his children to the size of ants. If Jesus is God's son and had an all-powerful, omniscient life ruling the universe, why would He want to shrink in size and prestige to join the insects?

Jesus took a serious demotion to show up on the planet as one of us. This downward mobility is unnatural in the scheme of human "progress." God must have been desperate to communicate with us directly—to show us that He understands what we go through, and to give us an example of how to be nice to one another.

When He was alive, Jesus had dirty, sandy, gritty feet; He had family issues; He knew what it was like to be caught between a rock and a hard place; one of His friends betrayed Him; people missed the point when He talked—all the human difficulties we experience. It's comforting to know that Jesus is the part of God who's been there, done that, and got the T-shirt.

Kingdoms in the Middle East come and go, shifting forever with the winds and sands of power. In Jewish history from Abraham to Christ, the Jews' united kingdom lasted only three generations before it split in two, and then both sides were hauled off in turn to Babylonia. The Israelites longed for their lost kingdom for centuries. By the birth of Jesus, they were chomping at the bit for a messiah, a military fighter to throw off the yoke of the Romans.

Surprise, surprise. God sent them a savior all right—Himself—but Jesus was a Messiah for an inner kingdom, not a political or military leader.

God has always cared more about conquering hearts than winning kingdoms.

In contrast, we humans love kingdoms, especially when the

kingdom is ours. We fight academic and corporate battles for tiny kingdoms, we go to war with deadly weapons for bigger kingdoms, and every family has its royalty, in terms of fighting for power and who gets to pick the family vacations. We pray to God to WIN whatever battle we find ourselves engaged in—territory, promotions, awards, you name it.

When God created people, He had companions for Himself in mind. He gave us a splendid place to live and said, "It's all yours." The problem is, God didn't want puppets or slaves; He wanted love.

Anyone who's reached adulthood knows that you can't force someone to love you. Ask the Phantom of the Opera. Threats don't work, bribes don't work, wheedling doesn't work, stalking doesn't work, and being somebody you're not doesn't work. The biggest Christmas present God left under the tree in the garden of Eden was choice. Adam and Eve opened the package and said, "We want to be the boss of ourselves. We want to know as much as God."

A brief overview of the death, destruction, violence of the world (not to mention the petty meanness, paltry power, and anger at the individual level) shows exactly how well self-control and the knowledge of good and evil has worked out for the human race.

God must sigh deeply watching our cutthroat antics in the race to the top of whatever anthill is in sight. The race to the moon. The race for the latest weapons. The race to be a millionaire. The race to have the highest sales, to get the teaching award, the prize. *As a species, they've missed the point. Even my chosen ones.*

What to do? God could have sent another flood to wipe out the problem of evil, but He'd promised not to do that again. God could have splintered the earth into a thousand meteors and flung us all into outer space. He could have written across the sky like the witch in *The Wizard of Oz* in words we all could read. He could have raised and trained holy people to warn the others that they were on the wrong track—actually, He did, but we see how effective the prophets were. Finally, God decided to pay us a visit Himself and pitch His tent among us.

Knowing well how the big boss of any large organization inspires fear, fawning, and infatuation (but not love), God decided not to swoop down as a mighty king. Instead, He came to earth as low man on the totem pole.

A few got it at first, especially after seeing Jesus around after He died. Then large numbers began to get it: God had come to earth to save us.

Late at night in seminary, armed with chips and a Dr. Pepper, I struggled through theology. I would probably have flunked except for a small group leader with an IQ way north of normal, who had the patience of Job and more.

Good grief! What was God thinking? What mere mortal can grasp a God who is a Father, a Son, and a Spirit? Three in one?

In seminary, I pored through wheelbarrows filled with words on the Trinitarian Godhead. All I remember from reading bushels of books are two images. First, water. One substance, but three manifestations. We drink water in a liquid form; we boil it and steam comes out the kettle spout as vapor; then we freeze it into hard ice cubes.

The other image is an apple. One apple with the same DNA throughout, but you have the skin, the seeds, and the flesh—three distinct parts.

My more intellectually astute seminarian classmates looked down on these explanations as being too simplistic, and they are, I agree. However, I have continued to cling to these analogies for dear life because they help explain the most complicated relationship in heaven or on earth—and without them, I'd drown, instead of swimming, in the Mystery of God.

5

But You Can't See Music

O Holy Spirit, descend plentifully
into my heart. Enlighten the dark
corners of this neglected dwelling
and scatter there Thy cheerful beams.
—St. Augustine

MANY ARTISTS DON'T PAINT without it. Students don't like to study without it. A dance isn't a dance without it. It can bring back the past in poignant, pleasant clouds of memory; it can make you cry; it can make you march to war.

From the back of the blue station wagon, my two-year-old son sang to the Disney cassette with gusto. When we pulled into the garage, I turned off the tape. He piped up from his car seat, "You know what, Mommy? I like music."

"I know, and you sing very well."

"But Mommy, you can't see music."

The Holy Spirit—the third person of the triumvirate of God—is a lot like music. You can't see it, but you know when it's there. It makes a difference.

In our own mind-body-spirit triad as humans, the spirit is hard to pin down. A look in the mirror, and you can't miss your body (with the same darn extra five pounds around the middle that you've carried for the last ten years). The mind? A steady march of words from the mouth gives away the mind. But spirit?

As the breath of life, our spirits animate us, keep us alive. During the last days of a friend's life, a small terrier named Cowboy lay across Danny's legs. When Danny stopped breathing, Cowboy got up, moved away, and hung his head over the side of the bed, while the nurses scurried around fooling with the machines, trying to resuscitate Danny. Cowboy knew. Danny's spirit had gone.

A person's spirit can be a dominating characteristic ("Uh, oh. Here comes Aunt Matilda. She's such a grump."), a motivating force ("You should read his latest book. It will make you want to get out of the recliner and conquer the world"); an essence, an inspiration, a feeling you get when you're around him or her.

This invisible quality leaks out in our actions, whether we know it or not. Human spirits attach to each other at a subliminal level: The esprit de corps of a supper club, the oneness of sharing with a spouse, the "click" one feels over a new friend. A teacher walks into the classroom on the first day, and no matter what's on the syllabus, students feel an immediate "great," or "I'd better get the heck out of here because this prof is a jerk."

And locations—the spirit of a place can kindle or repel us—an immediate inner reaction not based on anything but a feeling. Why does New York City with its energy, its art, its food make me tingle with the excitement of being alive, but driving across the desert in New Mexico (one of my husband's favorite trips) scares me and makes me feel lonely? Our spirits are hypersensitive instrument panels sending and receiving vibes from other people, from specific locations, and from situations. Things just "feel right"—or not.

I love the birth wing of the hospital, seeing the babies through the nursery window with scrunchy little ET faces. It's hard to tell one from another. Soon, however, parents know whether they are dealing with a sweet-spirited child, a howler, a placid baby, or a withdrawn infant. Spiritual connections form long before words.

The life of the spirit doesn't involve hocus pocus, or "weird," or spooky make-believe. Charlatans try to turn normal intuition into something hokey. We were created with a natural spiritual dimension, an exciting and valuable feature that can relate to a Higher Power and accomplish amazing things.

True examples: knowing someone's need before they express it. Having an inner voice say, "It's going to be all right" right after you get the word that a close relative has died. Overcoming an addiction. Having a sixth sense nudge you toward an unlikely job that turns out to be what you were looking for all along. Forgiving an abusive parent. Knowing the person you just met is your soul mate.

The spiritual world is the invisible web of signal transmissions wrapping around the globe like a skein of string; we are surrounded by hidden connections with each other and with the larger spiritual world. Forces for darkness and forces for light transmit in wavelengths we pick up at a subliminal level.

Like it or not, spirituality is part of the human package.

I have always been a practical person, and for practical people, the Holy Spirit can be the vaguest of all the manifestations of God: God in the fog. We understand God the Father because we know fathers, and Jesus was a real person who can relate to our bunions, bad hair days, and issues with neighbors, because He was once a human Himself. But the Holy Spirit.

The best way to grasp the Holy Spirit is when He grasps us first—by being blown away by the breath of God into a place of what I call "the deep wow," the bottom of the soul, the cavern of being.

Now for some factoids: The term holy spirit isn't unique to the Christian God. The Jewish spirit of YHWH roars like a wind, uprooting mountains, or alights on people like King Solomon or the Israelites as they made their mad dash through the Red Sea's opening.

But the Jewish holy spirit isn't God.

The Islamic holy spirit enlivened Adam and inspired Gabriel and breathes life in our mothers' wombs.

But the Muslim holy spirit isn't God.

The Baha'i faith, an off-shoot of Shiite Islam, believes that the holy spirit inspires humanity's great benefactors, teachers, and philosophers as an energizing force.

But the Baha'i holy spirit is not God.

The question hangs in the air like a limp helium balloon the day after a party. Why are the Christians so picky and insistent that God has three persons with one identical substance? Almost everybody believes that there's a good, inspiring force out there, a spirit of life—like good karma or a Higher Power. So why not leave it at that?

Before missionaries, the early African Sotho tribe went gaga over God the creator, the maker of all rocks, the rock itself that withstands the fire, the lord of heaven's vault. Holiness surrounded them in the jungle, a force too deep for the "measure stick."

As humans, our organs of perception are limited. In spite of what small children think about their mothers' instincts, we don't have eyes in the back of our head for a 360 degree view of the world. We can't hear sound frequencies that dogs can hear. Even the smartest person who ever lived had a capped IQ. Though people like the Sothos saw God's handiwork in the cathedral of the forest, nobody could see God.

So God fixed the situation. God decided to show up on the planet for a thirty-three year life span—where people could *see* Him and *hear* Him and *understand* what He said with our limited resources.

When He ascended back to heaven, people missed seeing Him, talking with Him. They didn't want a distant deity. So, God arrived again on the planet, this time as the Holy Spirit (who'd actually made a few special appearances to select people before landing as a dove on Jesus at His baptism).

The Holy Spirit's big debut to the rank and file occurred at Pentecost: a huge get-together, when the heavens poured out on a horde of people, becoming available to anyone who asked for it.

The enormous jostling and curious crowd experienced a great rush of wind, tongues of fire, and the unexpected ability to speak and understand different languages. Startled, the mob did not disperse and walk home, trying to minimize, or forget what must have been quite the show.

No. No, the mob became inflamed with the love of God, burning in the center of their lives.

Everything changed.

How do we know this is true? How can we be sure this occasion wasn't just gossip run rampant?

We don't. We can't. But there are a few hints, including the fact that Pentecost is still celebrated, while most of the other rumors of that era have died out.

The crowd ran about three thousand people. If only a handful had felt the spirit, the cynics would have won the day and quashed the hearsay. Instead, the Holy Spirit ripped through the Roman Empire as fast as word of mouth could travel—while the emperors tried to stamp it out by killing hundreds of thousands of Christians.

Most people aren't willing to get torn apart by lions in a near-naked state or get shot at with a hundred arrows or stabbed or beheaded or hanged or burned alive for something that hasn't exploded in the center of their being, turning their lives inside out. The martyrs became the accelerant for a growing conflagration of believers, passing the light from person to person, house to house, city to city.

Finally, the Emperor Constantine, looking for a god who would back his military prowess, received a vision, a dream and the sign of the cross: "By this sign you will conquer." Christianity had reached the power structure.

Over the next thousand years, the church moved from clandestine meetings in people's homes to the Great and Mighty Institution, an octopus-like organization centered in Rome and Constantinople, spreading its tentacles to the far reaches of the known world. With a few exceptions of truly holy men, the popes and patriarchs seemed more interested in conquering emperors and browbeating them into submission than in the salvation of souls.

But the Holy Spirit continued to burn, giving the church people like Teresa of Avila and St. Francis—who wanted a spiritual faith, shunning the folderol of the monstrous money-making machine of the church.

Reform, inside and outside the church, is a sign of the Holy Spirit bringing His wayward people back to God.

Because we are wayward. We humans tend to let power go to our heads. And when it does, look out. The Holy Spirit slides right out the back door and things tend to go haywire.

More often than not, the local nightly news is the nightly horror show: dogs attacking babies; parents smothering their children to death; new virulent viruses; plane crashes; and stories of the recent class of psychopath our culture has spawned, classroom killers shooting dozens at a time. With evidence of such evil, how can we know the Holy Spirit hasn't abandoned the earth to those who'd blow it up in a nuclear frenzy, those who'd hog all the food, those who'd let global warming burn us all to crispy smithereens?

Because besides the spiders we also have the fireflies. Because not everyone is careless about the poor, the struggling, or our planet's plight. Because unselfish leaders arise in every generation. Because the church is still plugging along.

And because it's difficult to argue with personal experience. The libraries of the world overflow with biographies and autobiographies of stone-cold atheists who've been grabbed and snatched by the Holy Spirit and changed forever. The experience is better than drugs. The buzz reaches down to the toes, and the high brings a peace and joy beyond description.

No matter what the nightly news touts, the Holy Spirit is still a force more powerful than death. Around 159,960 Christians are martyred for their faith every year. Yes, now. Two thousand years down the pike, people in other countries are still willing to die rather than relinquish the power of their beliefs.

The Holy Spirit is alive and well.

My phone is smarter than I am. It can take pictures, make videos, send e-mail, connect with Facebook, look things up on the Internet, play games, and get directions when I'm driving around lost. I can talk to my phone and it pays more attention to me than most of my students. I can punch a couple of buttons and chat with someone halfway around the world. The only thing my phone doesn't do is cook dinner.

Unfortunately, (in spite of my children's best efforts to teach me), the only thing I use my phone for is to talk, play two games, and yes, my latest accomplishment—text.

My phone is underutilized.

Much like the Holy Spirit.

For years, I didn't get it. The Holy Spirit was part of the God bundle, but I wasn't sure what this famous hallowed "Ghost" did, actually. Then I decided to pray to the Holy Spirit one afternoon in the doctor's office, while lying in one of those fashionable (ha) backless hospital tops, freezing, shivering, and terrified.

"Just get me through this procedure, please." Those were all the words that I could muster, but they were all I needed. After a minute or two, my body relaxed (no, it wasn't anesthetic drugs in the IV), and I felt a peace like warm honey flowing through my veins—a peace that certainly passed understanding, considering the circumstances.

The procedure was still painful, and the outcome didn't alleviate the problem, but I was calm inside. I thought, I'll have to try that again. After all, the Holy Spirit isn't called "The Comforter" for nothing.

Without sounding like Uncle Clyde the drunken pessimist, I admit that there is only one inescapable certainty in this life on earth: suffering (everyone suffers)—and death, of course. Everything else—love, happiness, parents who care, enough food to eat, friends, transportation, affection, success, health—all these are the extras, bonuses we've come to expect in America as entitlements...but the world doesn't promise these goodies. Instead the world's list of likelies goes like this:

Not being made of plastic (at least until we have knee replacements), our bodies will give us pain at times.

At least one friend will abandon or betray us.

We won't get a perfect job, spouse, house, or child.

Family members will die on us.

We will lose money.

Cars will wreck.

Taking these things as the given bedrock of life in the world, how is it possible to have a happy life? What can you do? Focusing on the Bad Thing—stewing about it, magnifying it, using it as the fishhook to dredge up other Bad Things in the Past—is not the answer.

Tragedies travel in packs. It's best to plan life's route around these roaming beasts (that is, purchase insurance, avoid bad investments, buckle your seat belt), but in spite of the best-planned itinerary, no one escapes them completely. Dreading them only gives them a scent on the trail; trying to escape makes them run faster.

Watching people you love suffer is even worse than your own suffering. After praying for the Bad Things to go away, sometimes the prayer is answered No. The pain escalates.

This is the point where bitterness, doubt, anger start circling like vultures over whatever faith you had. If things get bad enough, they swoop down and start pecking, and the next thing you know, the old belief system becomes a carcass.

Trust me. Been there.

Back to the good old serenity prayer is best—acceptance. But acceptance comes hard because we each have an innate sense that *things shouldn't be this way.* Yet they are.

However, I've learned a little secret and it has to do with the Holy Spirit. When I can look the Bad Thing in the face and tell myself that (1) God isn't picking on me, (2) if I'm going to enjoy the highs in life, I have to accept the lows, because those are the rules for living on a flawed planet, (3) nobody escapes from tragedy, and (4) God loves me in spite of the fact that He allows the Bad Thing to continue, then I can pray to the Holy Spirit to help me deal with it.

Sometimes this means helping me to get out of bed.

Sometimes this means helping me let go of my fury (justified though it might be, and, of course, from my own biased perspective, usually is).

Sometimes this means giving me the guts to get through the thing I dread most.

Sometimes this means asking for wisdom to see the situation from a different point of view.

Sometimes this means asking for patience (yes, the miserable quality that has ruined every timetable I've ever had for my personal life agenda).

Sometimes this means getting through a funeral, and the year, or ten, afterward.

Sometimes this means asking for a friend to hunker down with until the disaster goes away.

The Holy Spirit is the power surge, the salve, the mainstay, the companion.

As the bumper sticker reads, "Sometimes He calms the storm; sometimes He calms the person in the boat."

Over the years, I have lost interest in theme parks—Sea World, Six Flags, Disney World, with loud music, and sweaty, pushy mob scenes—as well as sports events with parking lots that take longer than thirty minutes to escape from; crowded, boozy parties where I know only three people and I'm married to one of them; and phone conversations that last an hour or more.

The Holy Spirit is the power surge, the salve, the mainstay, the companion.

In contrast, I've developed an interest in grandchildren (those cute little self-contained entertainment centers), art, and, (what is strange for a formerly crazed Energizer bunny whacked out on to-do lists), a spiritual life. Sitting, just sitting, has never been a highly prized activity, and maybe it's just that I'm getting old, but sitting has a new appeal. Mostly because I'm not sitting alone. There's a conversation going on, whether I'm forming any words in my head or not. Just asking the Holy Spirit in has changed everything.

I read recently about the Vatican's Head of the Observatory, Jesuit Father Jose Gabriel Funes, who believes that God could easily have created other life forms. Out of a hundred billion galaxies, each with hundreds of billions of stars—the math is beyond me—what are the chances that our sun alone has one orbiting planet capable of sustaining life?

Funes says we can't put limits on God. Further, these other life forms may have stayed in perfect relationship with their Creator—not chosen to rebel. They could be leading perfectly lovely and easy lives in their own garden of Eden, not riddled with sin, self-interest, and evil.

If so, then beam me up, Scotty.

In the meantime, God has sent us the Holy Spirit to help get us through life on this planet. Life in the Holy Spirit has its own set of certainties very different from the world's expectations:

Joy alights like a flock of butterflies, when you least expect it.

Reconciliation becomes an option.

Carrying the boulder up the hill like Sisyphus is no longer your lifelong task.

Love blossoms like an English garden—not in tight formations, but wild, everywhere, and shot through with color.

Beating yourself up for past mistakes is no longer your favorite pasttime.

You become a warrior, not a worrier.

Persistence in prayer—as in the hymn "How Firm a Foundation"—will "sanctify to you your deepest distress." This process may take a lifetime, but what better way to spend a life than overcoming whatever agony has landed on you or been planted by parents, circumstances, or crummy choices?

The best news about the Holy Spirit is that when God connects with our spirits, He is with us wherever we are—in jail or crying our eyes out or standing by the side of the road lost or sitting in a chair. When God doesn't seem to be answering our prayers, we can ask to *feel the presence* of the Holy Spirit. Even if the outward circumstances don't change, that prayer is almost always answered, later if not sooner.

Talking it out with the Holy Spirit is the best way to vent, to find direction in life, to heal from the world's wounds, to gain strength to carry on, to help forgive, to thrive, to dance with joy, and to relish the peace that passes understanding.

The Holy Spirit offers one more thing. As my friend Bea Brock put it, "The ultimate manifestation of the Holy Spirit is interconnectedness." We are not called to live in isolation, even if we're happy, sitting around feeling good about ourselves.

Loneliness is a spur to get us out and connect with our fellow travelers trudging down the road carrying loads of unresolved issues, anger, woundedness, fear, loneliness, low self-esteem, you name it.

We smile and wave at each other on this road of life, keeping our loads hidden from each other, afraid we are the only one suffering, instead of sharing the load.

Living in the Holy Spirit means help is available, to give or to receive. Living in the Holy Spirit means that we can be and meet up with God wearing skin, giving real hugs, bringing real food to each other.

Living in the Holy Spirit means we're all in it together. This is good news.

6

Potluck Suppers and Other Worship Opportunities

I see the church as a field hospital after battle.
—Pope Francis

AS THE ATTENTIVE READER WILL HAVE picked up by now, I love bumper stickers. Their pithy wisdom may reflect the essence of American life better than the history books—maybe not the facts, but the spirit. This sign posted on the back of a truck pretty well sums up the church. "The church is a hospital for sinners, not a hotel for saints."

Looking in from the outside, the church in the West has a few, well, issues. I can't tell you how many times someone has told me, "I don't like the church. I visited three different churches, and not a single person greeted me."

"One of the deacons is a mean person."

"I know for a fact that the pastor isn't truthful."

"They pray from a book. It's boring."

"They don't pray from a book. Prayer is an undignified free for all."

"They sing campfire music, not the classic hymns."

"Their music is stuck in the 1700s and doesn't relate to today."

"They're a bunch of self-righteous prigs. Hypocrites."

The problem with church is that, from the outside, it looks like it's filled with people who have trouble getting along.

That's because the church is filled with people who, yes, have trouble getting along —sinners—some who remember they aren't perfect, and some who've forgotten. And, like the nightly press coverage and gossip, it's mostly the bad stuff that makes the headline news. A thousand acts of kindness, self-sacrifice, and generosity are overlooked in favor of one sensational story about a minister or priest who dallied with youngsters—which is a terrible thing, but it isn't the only thing going on in the church.

Early Christians were hunted down and killed. As a result, congregations tended to meet and worship secretly in large private homes—not in the catacombs of Rome (although they did conduct burial services there). Churches did not put notices in the local papers advertising times of services. No, the early church usually met in the evening for a meal, with remarks and readings and Communion afterwards.

Problems in the early church did not include declining numbers. Or people only half-committed. Or people attending for social reasons. Traveling by word of mouth, the new faith drew people like a feeding frenzy. Starved for good news, people joined the church in mass numbers, even though joining the church was not easy. Not only did the threat of death hang over the heads of new converts, these catechumens had to undergo a three-year course before they could be baptized—plus they had to make a *public* confession of their sins.

Early church members had every excuse not to attend. Yet they came in droves.

Predicaments in the early church included some of the same old, same old problems of human nature, as well as unique quirks in getting a new institution off the ground. For example, the early church had no New Testament. No Gospels, only memorized stories and statements of Jesus. The letters of Paul came in the mail, fresh from his pen.

Once the apostles started dying out, the church had to decide who would be the chief supervisor in the churches they'd established. How would bishops, presbyters, and deacons get chosen? Elections? Drawing lots, like the twelfth apostle who replaced Judas?

This is not to mention music or liturgy. Who got to pray out loud? What happened when someone hogged the spotlight? Did Gentiles, people who weren't God's chosen ones, have to become Jews first before they could become Christians?

All these matters had to be hammered out, with people on different sides, arguing. And people then liked to win disputes as much as people do now. So the early church thrashed it out, creating a living institution instead of the Tower of Babel.

Paul's letter to the Corinthians gives us a picture of an early church assembly. People gathered at the house of a wealthy person willing to take the chance that the authorities wouldn't storm the house and arrest everyone. Around supper time, men and women trickled in, bringing individual wine and food for their own meal. (Potluck suppers didn't arrive on the scene until sixteenth-century England.)

The problem was that a few wealthy people brought huge feasts, and the poorer people didn't—and they clumped in separate little cliques. To add to the divide, new pagan converts brought meat roasted on the idols' altars—anathema to the former Jews. By the time the working classes arrived late, the early birds were drunk.

When the service started, there was no bulletin or a prescribed order of worship. Maybe some music; maybe a story from Jesus' life; maybe a reading from the Jewish scriptures, the Old Testament; maybe a new letter from Paul, making the circuit of new churches; then prayers; and Communion.

People argued over leadership. The ones baptized by Paul felt superior because Paul was a big shot. The ones baptized by Apollos felt superior because Apollos was a golden boy speaker. The "elite" church members who spoke in tongues lorded it over the ones who didn't, even though the church visitors standing around the edges didn't have a clue what the people were saying. Histrionics ran rampant.

In short, people clashed over the same things that church members today clash over. The only difference is that now when people get mad, they can stomp out and find a new church from the array of different churches around the corner. Or start a new church or stay at home and watch TV evangelists.

Human nature being what it is, it's a wonder the church has survived its own congregations for two thousand years.

They didn't have the Myers-Briggs personality test in the first century, but you can bet it was a J personality type who said, "Hey, we have to get this religious movement organized." By the time Constantine legalized Christianity in 325 CE, a hierarchy worthy of any international corporation had already flowered—and grew over the next centuries like kudzu. The one holy catholic church lasted almost a millennium, until the East and the West split in 1054.

After the first great whack of the mighty oak, dividing the Roman Catholics from the Eastern Orthodox, the church spent the next thousand years splintering into thousands of fragments, split by theology, politics, tradition, and worship. From an institution that had held hegemony over every aspect of people's lives for almost fifteen hundred years, the church in its many-splintered form managed, finally, to learn a few important things—especially in the last centuries—as worship and faith became individual and personalized, and the church became a choice rather than a regulation.

The church learned that you didn't have to burn people alive who disagreed with you over theological doctrines like transubstantiation (which the average Joe and Josephine didn't understand anyway).

The church learned that government couldn't dictate what people believed. A state-imposed religion only padded the wallets of those in charge and filled the pews with large numbers of people who attended out of fear.

The church learned that ultimately, faith is a one-on-one decision, and can't be forced down anyone's throat.

Now that we've entered the third millennium of Christianity, the culture has also learned a few things regarding the church. You can't eradicate faith—through indifference, through legalized atheism, or by writing books proclaiming God's death, as if saying so makes it true. Africa is burning up with new converts, and even in the United States, the Emerging Church movement has been as popular as Starbucks.

And Russia. The USSR tried to eradicate Christianity, outlawing worship and using the cathedrals as warehouses for grain. Yet, when times got tough in World War II, and the people had to fight against the invading Nazis, who did the government call in to strengthen and fortify the people? Not the Communist leaders, but the priests—taken out of captivity to pray, hold services, and encourage the people in their faith.

The Communist regime was an experiment in forced atheism, and it failed. Now the Russian church is back full throttle, having idled on the sidelines for almost a century. Western culture is no longer under the thumb of the church; rather the multiculturalists and political correctness mavens are the ones guiding popular thinking these days. And yet, in spite of laws against public prayer, God is still on our dollar bills, in our Pledge of Allegiance, and the church continues to be a place where people find comfort, fellowship, and the Holy Spirit.

The bad news about church history is that the Christian church exploded into a thousand fragments.

The good news about church history is that it's still the same God in charge of all the pieces.

Chaucer's inn and transportation service to Canterbury may not have had a five-star rating, but his tales do give us a five-star picture (the good, the bad, and the ugly) of the pre-Reformation Roman Catholic church. *The Prologue to the Canterbury Tales* immortalizes church "types" still found today, although not in such rich or salacious detail.

We meet the hoity-toity Prioress trying to be all that; the "manly" Monk who preferred riding fine horses to reading the Bible; the pimpled, slit-eyed Summoner, who milked the system; the slimy Pardoner, who tricked people into buying their way out of hell. We also meet the Parson, a good man who made sacrifices for his faith and tried to lead his flock to God.

A contemporary version of a church pilgrimage would include some similar personality types. Any church is speckled with the holy, the not-quite-so-holy, the holy wannabes, and the people who just want to be seen there. On any given day, I am all of the above, so I'm not in a position to judge the people sitting around me.

For centuries in the Anglican Church, citizens of England were hatched, matched, and dispatched in Anglican baptism, weddings, and funeral services, unless one took active steps to opt out. Anathema to our forebears, this principle formed the basis of America's decision to separate church and state. Church in the United States has always been a choice, in theory anyway.

The same year we moved from Oklahoma to Indiana, at age ten, I went to a Quaker meeting, during which the most entertaining thing for me was scratching my mosquito bites in the silence. The same year a friend took me to a Pentecostal service, which provided all kinds of fun: action was a central feature, with people slain in the spirit, shouting Amen, and flipping back and forth decorated fans from the local funeral home. At one point my friend and I slipped out and rode the wide curved banister from the second floor to the first.

Church in America is like having 2,875 channels on cable. One click of the button, and you're in a whole different worship world—from stained glass to storefront, from prayer book to big screen, from house church to auditorium.

When looking for a place to worship, it's best to ignore the labels.

Churches that used to be called "mainstream" (Methodist, Presbyterian, Lutheran, etc.) over and against "catholic" or "evangelical" now contain branches within each, and the "social action" branches or the "inclusive" branches or the "fundamentalist" branches have more in common with each other across denominations than within.

Congregations in African churches dance, sing, and pray through seven-hour services. Seven hours on a Sunday? Yes. In Uganda, it takes seven hours to confirm all the new members eager to join the church.

Why the boom? Postcolonialism disparages the early missionary movements as oppressive, but out of these missionaries' mangled or misguided efforts, something took hold. Nowadays, no one is forcing these throngs of people to join the church.

All I can say is, institutions, like empires, rise and fall, but the Holy Spirit is never ending. When one church forgets its original purpose and becomes a victim of lethargy, entropy, or loss of interest, another church springs up.

The early church expected Jesus to return in a flash; the later church has realized that *kairos* is not *chronos,* and a minute in God's time is a thousand years in ours.

Church history is pocked with examples of Christian behavior we'd rather delete than remember (the Inquisition, for example), but history is also filled with Christians behaving well (the abolitionist movement, the Salvation Army).

The difference between a philanthropy and a church is that a church is called to love the least of these, not just to give them money or leftover coats. Secular foundations and churches both reach out to those in need and do great work in the world. Both can feel good about making a difference.

The church, though, operates from a different stance. Foundation members give from excess; church members often give until it hurts because they know a secret that secular society doesn't: everything we have comes from God. Yes, we work hard for what we get, but ultimately—and this applies not to just our money and sophisticated junk, but our very existence—*everything* depends on God, who gives us another day to live even if we wake up cranky.

So the church gives and does things for others, whether we want to or not. In the deepest giving—the cheering crowd and the applause come not from the world, but from Jesus. Everyone pays a price to be who we are, but obedience to God's call costs us everything.

However, the reward is also everything. The church is a place where people hand out water bottles and cheer each other on in the marathon of life, as we run for a cause greater than ourselves. When we fall and break a leg, or when a bomb goes off as it did during the Boston marathon, the church is a place we can come to lick our wounds and weep together for the fallen.

The church is family, where Thanksgiving dinner may turn into a battle of wills, but at least you know you have a place at the table. When we're at the bottom of a dry cistern; when we've run out of cash, friends, jobs and luck; when no one remembers our birthday; when we have trouble getting out of bed; the church is a place where God lives, where He hands out love like water, where we can go and sit, and thank Him for the trip, even when we think we don't have anything else to thank Him for.

Because here's the difference between the church and any other secular group in the postmodern civilization: our culture screams at us that happiness equals possessing. Who could be happy if enemy bombs destroyed our homes, our cars, our technology, our way of life? What if we had no shelter except what we could build with our hands, no food except what we could grow, and no way to get anywhere except by walking?

This picture is our historical past, more recent than we'd like to think, and is still the reality today for more people on earth than not. Not only do most people not have three-ply toilet paper, they don't have toilets.

We started this life with the skin on our backs. Everything since then has been a gift. The culture trains us to be discontented. The church trains us to be grateful. One can never underestimate the power of a church service, where people pray for each other and provide a place where we're reminded that we already possess the pearl of great price, even if we've just lost our house.

Flying into New York City is a good reminder that higher perspectives do exist. When native tribe leaders were first taken up in an airplane, the pilot pointed out their village, with their huts. The native tribe leaders refused to believe it was their village because the aerial view looked nothing like the view from the ground; from above, the huts looked like circles not structures with doors.

Even when Christianity meant very little to me and the world meant a lot, I enjoyed going to church. Go figure. I'm still a church member now, even though, as the rector's wife, I've seen the church's underbelly and, yes, it has a bunch of barnacles on the bottom.

However, once I'd accepted that God has the airplane view of life and that He created me, not just one ant out of many; once I'd met Jesus Christ and experienced the power of the Holy Spirit, then—even if I'm reduced to living alone with a campfire in my backyard and a cardboard tent—I will feel impelled to worship, with gratitude, and to find others to sing praises with me.

I once heard in a sermon Elie Wiesel's story about a group of people sitting in a boat, and one man started creating a hole underneath his seat. The rest of the people said, "Wait! You can't do that. If you crack the wood, we'll all drown." The man replied, "It's my seat. I can do what I want with it."

In the church, we are all in it together.

7

Whose Life Is It, Anyway?

Houston, we have a problem.

OUR FAVORITE DESIGN-YOUR-OWN pizza place lets you select the perfect pizza by choosing ingredients, sauce, and crust out of an amazing variety (Capers? Marinated broccoli?). Voila! Fifteen minutes later your ideal, mouth-watering pizza miraculously appears on your plate, ready to devour.

If life were like a pizza, we'd all be happy, choosing the ingredients for our own personal banquet. One of the greatest gifts God has given us is freedom to choose.

Unfortunately, that freedom also extends to other people, and what others choose may turn out to be, heaven forbid, anchovies on a shared pizza (or, worse, they can poison our pizza). Other people's bad choices constitute the first problem with controlling our own lives.

The second problem with control is that sometimes we actually *don't* have a choice.

Ordering our own delicious life may be an illusion, but it's an illusion we cherish. Americans yearn from the pit of our national consciousness to believe that we are in control. That we can control our destiny, control the behavior of other countries, and, in fact, control the world. Individually, we believe that we can choose to create or destroy our own happiness with good or bad decisions and that we can accomplish the goals we set for ourselves.

Our lives belong to us. Right?

Like most great truths, this one has an escape hatch for exceptions. (Like saying, "Arizona has hot, dry summers," but visiting Phoenix the one weekend that it rains. Or saying, "America is the land of the free and the home of the brave." Yes, and yes, but not everyone was free when the song was written in 1814, and not everyone is free now, in bondage through prejudice, the sex trade, or economic handcuffs.)

How much control do we really have over what goes on in our little slice of the great pie? Whose life is it, anyway?

From the beginning, white Anglo-Saxon Americans wanted control of life as an assembly of states against England and fought a revolution to gain autonomy: "No taxation without representation." Our forebears got what they wanted. In the next century, America's "manifest destiny" may not have been manifest to the Native Americans, but it was destiny to everyone else, and we plowed across the country, again getting (or, rather, taking) what we wanted. Subservience is not part of our national character.

Power in the big picture—the national/international scene, either in politics, economics, sports, music, arts, or fame in general—requires (much of the time, but not always, of course) sophisticated social machinations, tireless and obsessive struggling, an iron will, a midget conscience, luck, blinders to both one's own competing desires as well as others' needs, and the greatest of all success-producing traits: persistence, persistence, persistence.

Yet, still, in every election, someone loses. For every executive appointment, someone else doesn't get the job. For every Super Bowl victory, one team goes home defeated. Controlling the world is for an elite few, and even for the rare sprinkling of those who scale to the top of their Mount Everest of choice, ultimately they don't control everything. Sometimes the spouses of world leaders leave them; the children of the rich and powerful sometimes hate them; politicians get voted out of office or wander off to die in oblivion; and death, the great equalizer, follows behind, sooner or later bringing loss of mind control, loss of willpower, loss of hope, and loss of unmentionable bodily functions before the final collapse.

Controlling the world is a job that belongs to a scarce handful—it is a fleeting job, and, perhaps, not as fulfilling as one would have hoped.

As the notion of control filters from the big picture into our individual lives, most of us still think we can get what we want, one way or another—if we're willing to pay the price, (or get someone else to pay the price for us). Because there's always a price tag for gaining control.

Most of us won't get to be president or powerful public figures, so we lower our sights to controlling our own small corner of the world, which is still a daunting task. Control over my life is an intimidating challenge to my faith in Christ. Since when does Jesus know what's best for me and those I love? As a child of an alcoholic, one of the first things I learned was to control everything I could get my hands on because I had no control over the biggies in life. With extensive personal study of the exercise of control, I'm providing here examples of the kind of petty control that doesn't work, that ruins relationships, and that goes against the whole point of godly love.

Aunt Matilda did not want to schedule the meeting at eight o'clock in the morning. She said to her four surviving siblings, "We simply don't need to get to the lawyer's office that early. It's ridiculous." Aunt Matilda wasn't accustomed to getting out of bed before eight.

Before she died, their mother had insisted that all five siblings be present, together, for the reading of the will. They voted four to one to meet at eight o'clock. Two of the sisters were from out of town and had planes to catch, their only brother had a nine o'clock meeting, so eight o'clock it was.

Aunt Matilda didn't care. She would not be bullied into inconvenience. Knowing they couldn't start without her, she appeared at 8:37 and not a minute sooner.

Control through selfish manipulation leads to resentment, even if you win.

Or: "Oh, my, dear. You're not going to wear that dress are you? I thought you wanted to make a good impression on this young man. The pink dress makes you look so much slimmer."

Control through veiled insults leads to resentment, even if you win.

Or: "I don't care where you decide to go to college, but I'm not paying a dime if you don't go to the state university, where I went. Where all your uncles went."

Control through blackmail leads to resentment, even if you win.

Or: "I'm sorry you've made plans to go to your husband's office party. I guess I'll have to hire someone with more flexibility if you can't stay late and finish the report. This is the third time you've tried to beg off on something I've told you to do."

Control through intimidation leads to resentment, even if you win.

Turns out, controlling those around us is a thankless task. Really, most of our friends, family, and coworkers don't appreciate our good intentions and don't recognize that we know what's best for them.

Control of other people usually means manipulation in disguise. Organized crime provides extreme examples of how to control other people. Control by getting rid of your enemy—quickly and efficiently—is, of course, the most effective means. Simply shoot troublesome people. Put them out of their misery. And yours. Kings, rulers, and other governments have a long history of this technique. It's called assassination, but it doesn't work well for friends and family.

Actually, controlling other people isn't all bad. Control of family members is important if they're under the age of eighteen, belong to you, and are misbehaving badly. For example, in the family SUV on Sunday:

"I want to go to McDonald's for lunch."

"I hate McDonald's. Dad, please. Let's go to Taco Bell."

"He always gets his way."

"Not true. Quit kicking the seat."

"He hit me!"

"Boys, stop it. Starting today, we will rotate who gets to pick Sunday lunch. Mom will go first, and then you'll each have a turn in order of age. I'll be last. This arrangement will continue until... until forever, until you die, or at least until you leave home. I'm sick and tired of the fighting. Got it?"

"Not fair, I'm the youngest, and—"

"But Dad—"

"You hate us."

Mom says, "That's enough. Today we are going to the fried chicken place, *unless one more person hits or complains*." Threatening glare from the front seat.

Control of other people is also important in war, during other life-threatening situations, and... well... that's about it. Let's face it, when other people don't do what we tell them to, it's a problem, even when we force the issue and they buckle. Controlling someone outside the boundary of a contract, implicit or otherwise, leads to resentment.

Here's what life has taught me: unless you enjoy collecting prickly, thorny bouquets of bitterness from people around you, the best thing to do is to work on controlling yourself. I've learned this valuable piece of information the hard way by trying to run others' lives. In fact, I continue to learn the hard way, when I spread what I think is dazzling wisdom, brilliant instruction, and proper guidance to grown family members, who, surprisingly, think that they know what's right for them. They are correct, of course, and they haven't shot me yet. You might say that my journey in faith has been a process of learning to relinquish control to a God who is much smarter, wiser, kinder, and loving than I am.

So what does it mean to relinquish control? How does one control oneself? For some this means resisting the urge to beat up people in bars; for others it means resisting the catty remark, learning how to have a civilized conversation when someone refuses to comply with what you want them to do. Most radically, it means letting other people be who they are and stop trying to make them into a better person, in your humble opinion. Even if your intentions are purely good.

Even if you think they'd be happier if only they'd just (fill in the blank).

The zeal of a determined do-gooder, like the zeal of a new convert, often resembles a blowtorch in people's faces rather than a candle lighting the way. No wonder they don't respond the way we think they should.

Controlling yourself is not nearly as much fun as controlling other people. The especially interesting part of control is that so much of it is unconscious. People pleasers control with niceness: "Oh, yes, but don't you think Mary would enjoy it more if we changed the date?" The secret agenda coated with sugar is a deadly weapon.

The bottom line in control issues is that, as the ad says, I DO want it my way. We each live in the center of ourselves, and others orbit around us. Therefore, we think we have the right—indeed, the obligation!—to get the planets in line with what our experience tells us is right.

What often never occurs to us, especially in getting older, is that the planets in our orbit see themselves as the sun, and *we are their planets.* Everyone we encounter thinks they are the center. Our children don't grow up to do what *we* want, but what *they* want. (How dare they!) On the other end of the sandwich generation, our parents dig in their heels, determined to stay in their homes until long past the time we think they should enter assisted living. Everywhere we go, other people think they are the center of the universe: the salesgirl, for instance, is more interested in flirting with the stock boy than in paying attention to me, the customer.

Each of us has a control room, dead center in our lives. This room is where information from the mind meets sensory body data and converges with emotions produced from what we perceive goes on around us. This life center, the place of integration, used to be called the soul because it is a spiritual place—the hub, the core, the "heart" of our humanness.

Who or what controls the control room is essential. Memories from childhood, chemicals from the brain, praise from mentors, self-talk, accidents, failures, successes—the control room takes input from everywhere, sorts it, and spits out attitudes that influence how we go about our lives.

If self-desire is the dominant trait in the control room, then we're probably headed for disappointment because other people are trying to control their own lives—and us—and relationships become like bumper cars.

Fortunately, human beings are not concrete statuary. At the center of the human organism is the ability to change and grow—again just ask the developmental psychologist Jean Piaget. One of the crucial stages is the giant leap that children take from egocentrism to decentering. Egocentrism is the girl who says, "Because I like to play dress up, Daddy must like to play dress up, too." After decentering, children can look at life and other people through other perspectives, and sooner or later the girl can say, "I like to play dress up, but Daddy likes to play golf."

However, people who go through a traumatic experience during that developmental period can get stuck, self-centered for life; their world view is skewed, and instead of understanding life from another perspective, they develop a fierce (that is, pathological) need to control other people, to force others to accept their point of view as the ONLY one. People with this narcissistic tendency become outraged when other people don't comply. It feels to them like rejection.

We all know people like this. They are not centered; they have god-complexes; they are not comfortable in their own skin; they develop a disorder.

Sometimes the enemy is us, trying to run the universe.

Control starts early, the moment a newborn emerges, takes a deep breath, and wails—terrorized and flailing in the harshness of light and air. Newborns don't have many tools at their disposal, but they have a set of lungs, which is what they use to get what they need for survival: comfort through physical contact and food, two things they got effortlessly, automatically in the womb.

Now, suddenly, infants have to signal to get their needs met. Except in cases of neglect, infants cry and someone shows up to give them what they need. Cause and effect begin to form pathways through the trillion neurons in the brand-new brain: screaming brings relief.

So far, so good. Survival depends on this process, and trust is established if the infant has a reliable caregiver. The infant learns how to gain control over painful situations such as hunger pangs.

The problem occurs later. Whether it arrives like rosy-fingered dawn or a sledgehammer, something troubling occurs. The person with the food doesn't always show up on demand, and now the toddler has to wait until lunch is ready. The older sister pokes and pulls at body parts, and nobody stops her. Colic brings suffering. Unchanged diapers cause a rash. Howling doesn't always bring the desired results. In fact, screaming is now sometimes discouraged or punished—by the same caregiver who used to orbit around the infant.

Deep inside from the get-go, the infant has developed the illusion of the way life is supposed to be—control over parents, and instant gratification. The person who gives in to every whim of a shrieking child (or adolescent, or spouse for that matter) only furthers the illusion that life entitles the child to control everything. Sooner or later, most of us suffer the reality that we are not princes and princesses, though the illusion dies hard.

I need to make a distinction here, one we all know but try to ignore—getting what we *need* is a life-force, a survival mechanism. Getting what we *want* isn't, and the fastest ticket to unhappiness is not learning the difference between what we can (and should) control and what we can't. Somewhere between infancy and adulthood, what we want morphs into what we need. Like *needing* the latest technology. *Needing* a bigger salary, a nicer house, a fancy car. You get the picture. This phenomenon leads straight to the bottomless pit syndrome, one of America's several diseases. We are more-machines.

Spoiled children who control their parents are not happy children. They grow into adults who suffer from ennui, discontent. The result of getting what you want by gosh, by golly, by stealth or by tantrums is not serenity but rather self-saturation topped with a little bit of "nanny nanny boo boo" pride, and strains from the song "I Did It My Way" poured over the top. But serenity was never the goal. Getting what you want was.

The serenity prayer for control addicts goes something like this: God grant me the ability to push all obstacles out of the way, to crush whatever I need to manipulate the world the way I want, and the guile to make everyone around me think I'm still nice.

The saying, "Let go and let God" is the bane of the control freak. Just ask me. I'm an expert, which is why writing this chapter is ironic—and rates a 9.9 out of 10 on the discomfort scale. Who wants to take a serious look at their own issues?

I guess I do, if I'm interested in my spiritual welfare.

So why does the need to control drain all the fun out of agendas, relationships, work, vacations, and all other situations within range of our radar? Who cares if we go to lunch before or after the business meeting? Who cares if we leave one day or the next? If we watch this on TV now and tape that for later?

On a larger scale, control goes to central issues. Getting a certain job matters to the center of our personhood, leading to pride—or shame. Controlling teenagers' behavior matters to our children's future and also to our self-esteem as parents (did we do the best we could?). The control room goes berserk when we are threatened by loss of control of something essential to the image of ourselves. No! No! He can't leave me! No! No! My daughter can't go to rehab! WHAT WILL PEOPLE THINK?

New Age "create your own reality" still has a pleasant ring to it, decades later. If only we could. If each of us lived in a bubble of our own making, the earth would be covered with suds. The problem, of course, is all those other slippery bubbles that sidle up to, and puncture, ours.

Like it or not, a certain amount of reality is shared. Or, at least we operate under the assumption that seven billion people besides us live on the same planet. Fact: most things are out of our control, though many people continue to live with the illusion that they can control their lives—if only they are elected. If only they make enough money or enough friends in the right places. Or if only they could get rid of the selfish Neanderthals in the way.

The triangle of control, illusion, and suffering is a three-pronged weapon guaranteed to create misery and despair in those who believe in its invincibility.

The definition of illusion is "a lie we want to believe."

The definition of control means "being in command."

The definition of suffering means "mental, spiritual, physical anguish."

Illusion leads to suffering, sooner or later. Presidents ride into office high on the illusion (delusion) that they can sweep in and accomplish all their promised goals. Marriages, business partnerships, friendships, programs of study, parenting, writing a book: people don't begin any of these relationships or activities thinking, This new situation is going to be the hardest thing I've ever done. I'm going to run into obstacles out of my control. No, the "happily ever after" syndrome surrounds expectations like fog on a mountain. "It's going to be great! A piece of cake! Things are going to go my way!" When the illusion of control grinds to a halt, stripped, like gears, of the ability to move the vehicle down the road, suffering is the result.

Standing helplessly by the side of the road (or in a pink-tiled shower) is the point at which the center either holds, or it doesn't.

When we were first married, Stockton and I volunteered to help the teacher in the two-year-old Sunday school class at church. I remember a vivid scene during free-play. Ethan and Kevin were playing with blocks on the rug, and Anne sat at a side table drawing a picture. Kevin spied one of Ethan's blocks (the only red block in the pile), grabbed it, and put it on the top of his tower. "Mine!" he gloated. Ethan howled in protest.

At this point, Anne looked up, saw her friend Ethan in pain and got up to console him by patting him on the shoulder. Not comforted by little Anne's gesture of kindness, Ethan continued to scream, wallowing in a puddle of outrage. Anne stepped back and stared at him, not knowing what to do. Then he lunged, tearing down Kevin's tower; Ethan hit Kevin and grabbed his red block, hugging it to his chest. Anne wandered back to the table.

Now Kevin started screaming and hit Ethan in return. Before blood was shed, the teacher separated the two. "No screaming. No hitting." She got another block and each child now had an identically shaped block, one red and one blue.

Kevin, however, still wanted Ethan's red block. He wanted to control the situation and wouldn't settle for a blue block. He again grabbed the red block. Ethan grabbed it back. Both children cried. Anne looked over, helpless, sucking her thumb.

Once more the teacher arrived on the scene. "Be nice," she said. "Share." She handed both of the toddlers a green block.

Undeterred, Kevin crawled back to the pile, where the teacher had placed the red block, took it, and started to build his tower again. "Mine," he told Ethan.

"No!" Ethan yelled back.

The teacher then lifted the two boys, placed each in a separate chair across the room from each other, and said, "Time out. Now go to your happy place inside."

This scenario is the history of the human race, repeated over and over and over, with more sophisticated language and progressively more deadly weapons—fists, then clubs, then spears, then catapults, then guns, tanks, bombs, missiles, and nuclear warheads instead of blocks. "I want to dominate" is the theme of human history, and those who offer aid (such as the Red Cross) take a secondary role, like Anne, who did what she could.

Control, illusion, suffering.

The desire to control our destiny, which includes ruling over the people (or nations) around us. The illusion that we can. The pain that comes when the illusion is shattered, often by war.

If the control room of a person is the intersection of the mind, body, and emotions, then—when we discover that we really can't control Uncle Clyde's drinking, we are forced to consider learning how to control *our response* to the difficult people and the unpleasant packages that life keeps leaving on our doorstep.

Take it from the teacher in the two-year-old classroom. First, she appeals to the body, what we can control physically: "No screaming, no hitting." Unfortunately, even adults get sucked into screaming back in response to mean people. On a personal level, we yell back at Uncle Clyde's drunken abuse, or on a global scale, we enter World War II.

When the toddlers can't control their physical responses, the teacher next appeals to their mental condition: "Be nice. Share." This attempt assumes that even the most sophisticated negotiator for world peace can control anyone else's mind and attitude, as Neville Chamberlain discovered September 1, 1939, when Germany invaded Poland. It takes two to dance the peace dance.

The human race has known how to define right and good and just for millennia, since the Greeks—so what's the matter with the human race that we can't construct an ideal republic, or even create a utopia that works for longer than a week, except on paper?

We can't. If we are angry with a neighbor whose dog leaves large souvenirs on our lawn, we want to even the score, to get control over the neighbor and his dog, so we won't have to deal with any more disgusting doggy doo on our property. This principle also holds true for nations and terrorist groups who decimate our skyscrapers.

The third level the teacher appeals to is emotions. She physically separates our two young, feisty combatants and says: "Go to your happy place." If we all lived in our happy place, then we wouldn't need the Home Owner's Association to settle disputes, the Supreme Court, Fort Leavenworth, or the United Nations.

But again, we can't. At least I can't. Too many people out there think they know what's best for me, for my children, for my husband, as well as the church—and these people who try to control their priest's wife (for my own good, of course) don't hesitate to tell me. According to a select few former parishioners who instructed me (unasked) how to parent, I was both too lenient and too strict during the same incident at church.

The problem is that others' unsolicited control upsets the balance in my happy place.

The only person I can control is myself, and the only way I can control myself is to ask a Higher Power to come get the malware out of the system. Strangling my husband's parishioners is not an option.

Unfortunately, we would prefer to work on improving our circumstances than ourselves.

The million-dollar question is, who's controlling the control room? Most of my life, it's been ME, ME, ME, with fear or anger or parental voices telling me what to do and who I should be. Besides selfishness and the inability to distinguish what I can control from what I can't, fear seems to be an override for whatever precarious systemic balance I manage to achieve in the soul.

As my husband so eloquently said in a sermon, fear of failure—in a career, in a marriage, in life—actually helps *create* failure by drawing all the magnetic particles to the center and clogging the machinery of the soul. When fear rules the control room, the human organism draws in on itself, develops porcupine spines for protection, corrodes positive energy, diminishes gifts and talents, and turns the air toxic, affecting everything we feel and think and do.

It's important to know what we can control and what we can't. We may be angry at Uncle Clyde's verbal abuse, but we don't have to throw the antique vase against the wall in response. We also don't have to stay angry for the next twenty-seven years until he dies. We can leave the room. We can forgive him. We can put something else in the center of the control room and be comfortable in our own skin again.

Here's the way it works: We can control our hairstyle, until our hair falls out from chemotherapy.

We can control what career we choose, until we get laid off.

We can control whom we marry, until they leave us.

We can control where we live, until we're evicted.

We can control how many children we have, until we get pregnant in spite of birth control, or until one of our children dies.

We can control our lives, until we can't.

And then we are lost without help.

Over the last sixty years, I have learned to accept help—the hardest thing for a control freak. People have given me insight and wisdom when I've asked. Friends and family have loved me no matter what.

Yet when I was standing in that pink shower stall, the center of me threatened to explode into a thousand pieces. God is the one who stepped in, with love, and said, "You lie down and rest. I'll take it from here."

We can control our lives, until we can't. And then we are lost without help.

The difference between heading into old age as a fine wine or rancid grape juice is the process of maturation, and maturing is the gradual relinquishment of control. To accomplish this life-task, prayer and practice are necessary, along with belief that God can actually wring clean water out of a dirty dishrag, but only if I let Him.

8

When I Was Young, I Bit My Sister, and That Was Just the Beginning of the Problems of Being Nice

Sin is a great thing as long as it's recognized.
It leads a good many people to God
who wouldn't get there otherwise.
—Flannery O'Connor

MY SISTER AND I WERE horsing around in the backyard after supper. She was six and I was eight, and a push here and a shove there led to a bite on my hand, which led to a bite on her arm—which in turn led to tattling in outrage to Mother the Judge, who sent us both to our room. *She bit me first,* I fumed in self-righteous indignation, ignoring the fact that it was barely a nibble on my ring finger, but it was a huge chomp I'd tried to take out of her upper arm.

We both remember the incident, fifty-six years later.

By kindergarten both my sisters and I had mastered the 1950 Southern girl's core philosophy: "Be Nice." Teachers loved us because we weren't any trouble. We had a repertoire of smiles—the friendly smile; the smug smile; the "I don't agree with you but I'm too polite to say anything" smile, and the withering "How can you be so stupid?" smile.

Our behavior was, in public, exemplary. We were nice girls.

The biting incident, however, has always been my touchstone for the hidden problems with being nice. Here is the rest of the story. First, I was already angry because Mother let my younger sister (and not me) stay with a friend for the second feature at the movies that afternoon. Because I was nice, I couldn't admit I was furious. So I smoldered through supper.

Second, after supper I picked a fight under the guise of "just playing around," pushing a little harder than necessary out in the backyard. Third, my sister responded beautifully by taking a nibble at my finger. Aha!—my opportunity for revenge—I sank my teeth into her arm. Finally, self-righteousness and justification because SHE BIT ME FIRST.

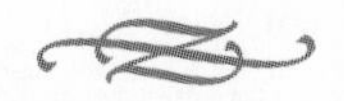

The word *nice* is like a newlywed's car, trailing strings of cans with different meanings behind it, all clanking with the same positive but hollow, superficial ring. "Pleasant." "Agreeable." "Genial." "Smooth." "Good."

A hostess asks, "How was the dessert?" "Nice," we respond because we don't want to admit that her gooey pudding reminded us of grade-school paste. Parents tell their children, "Be nice," when they mean, "Don't kill each other over a silly toy." "Nice job" means "passable but not spectacular"; "nice gift" means "thank you but I really didn't need a giant hedge clipper"; "nice shot" means "you're a turkey for acing me in tennis, but you're also my husband's boss's wife so I'm going to be a good sport." And so on, until the word's muscle tone becomes flabby and overextended, and *nice* becomes, essentially a meaningless term.

Caught in the talons of one of his young, sexy students in a spectacular flyover across the college's gossip field, the head of the business department was discussing his theology at a faculty get-together. His wife was a Christian, but she had lost her charm for him, and he had ditched both his faith and his family for a broader, more accepting belief system. When asked, he proclaimed that the key to his new faith was being "nice."

Afterward, one of the faculty members muttered, "Nice. Hmm. Who, exactly, considers him to be nice? The wife? The mistress? The children? Nice seems a little vague under the circumstances."

Though convenient for the person embracing the "nice" philosophy, being nice tends to break down under closer examination. Someone interviewing five candidates for a sought-after position can be nice, after all, to only one of them. Teachers are considered nice only if they give As and positive comments, ignoring gross errors on papers three weeks late. Parents are nice only if they praise their children and do not give consequences to violent or inappropriate behavior.

People clinging to the self-definition of "nice" are likely to wreak all kinds of havoc around them, trying to maintain the image of their own niceness.

According to the prevailing culture, being a nice person, like being a good person, is what gets you into heaven. Even Christians can get pulled into the quicksand of this notion. I lived in the quivering pit of goodness, my nose barely above the sand for decades, *determined* to be nice. Nice was my destiny. All I had to do was exert more effort.

I hated being nice. Nice meant pleasing everyone, an impossible and unrewarding task. Picking an activity with one friend over the other meant not being nice to one of them. Being nice is exhausting.

Take two parents hell-bent on winning the battle of shaping a "nice" child—one wants her daughter in the Junior League and the other is determined to raise a musician. Besides the fact that it isn't "nice" to use a child as a battleground, how can the child respond to the warring parents and still be nice? Which parent does she disappoint? And besides, she really wants to be an accountant, not a society belle or a pianist.

Being nice all the time means that eventually the real you disappears completely. All that's left are the bubbles on the surface of the quicksand.

The Twelve-Step programs call this self-consuming niceness "codependence" and have revealed it for the disease it is. Nobody can be nice all the time. Trying will eventually kill you.

The package of humanness includes the right to ourselves; the right to configure circumstances to our best ability; the right to select our own company when possible; the right to choose between wallowing in or making the best of a tragic situation; the right to make good moral choices, or not.

We all know about relative morality—take the common example of a boy who steals to feed his starving, orphaned sister, over and against the boy who steals to support his drug habit. The act is the same, but the morality behind the act differs.

With relative ethics comes a second skill set developed and perfected in our culture: self-justification. At the national level we have "justified" several wars, based on specious information about, say, enemy weapons of mass destruction. What we really wanted was to get someone back for taking down the World Trade Center and attacking us on our home territory. So we justified a war.

On an individual level, our justification gymnastics rival the torques and gyrations of the national Olympic team. We make decisions all the time, claiming that we have the other person's best interest in mind, when deep down, the outcome is what *we* really want. We lie (telling ourselves that no one will find out, and besides the truth would surely be harmful); we steal (we deserve it—they'll never miss it); we covet, we lust, we swear, and my personal favorite, we gluttonize, gorging on peanut butter cups, dark chocolate, and bread and butter, feasting at all-you-can-eat buffets, taking seconds so as not to hurt the hostess's feelings—all the while justifying the orgy with self-promises of a diet in the vague future and an inner reminder that not all fat is bad for the body.

Self-justification is like Gumby, who can be bent into any shape whatsoever. Rationalization is our most handy human tool to avoid unnecessary and irritating feelings of guilt when we know we've crossed a line.

A cousin to self-justification is self-righteousness. The three most treasured words in the English language are apparently not *I love you*, as many may think, but rather *You were right*. We are a nation craving to be right, to be the winners in any argument. We slunk out of Vietnam and took our national losses out on the boys who came home by ignoring their service to a country who was not right in the end, who did not win the war. Being right is often a rickety scaffolding.

The difficulty about being right in all arguments is that since the drive to be right often eliminates the possibility of creative compromise (along with respecting other opinions), the self-righteous person ends up surrounded by people who have lost the discussion, the decision, the prize—people, in fact, angry at being put down. People who don't like us. Knowing it all, not admitting mistakes, trumping every conversation with a better story may make us feel good about ourselves, but ultimately leaves us friendless and lonely.

Niceness, justification, and being right, as it turns out, have a darker side. We don't feel as good as we expected.

Niceness, justification, and being right, as it turns out, have a darker side. We don't feel as good as we expected.

Sin is such a dirty word—unpopular, outdated, misused. Several decades ago, Karl Menninger wrote a book about how the word *sin* simply vanished from the American culture like the magician's rabbit in a poof of denial.

Erasing the word from our national vocabulary at first brought cultural relief. If sin no longer exists, then we are no longer guilty. However, in the long run, Menninger discovered the corollary for a wholesale jettison of sin, the part of our human nature that nobody wanted—an increase of mental illness.

Outdated according to many, the church nevertheless has provided a system for dealing with what we used to call "sin," a cycle of forgiveness and renewal after being sorry for doing wrong. With the eradication of "wrong," and the postmodern meta-narrative that "anything goes," we are stuck, as human beings, with unidentified shadows we can no longer name. When we called errors, immorality, mistakes, evil, and selfishness "sin," we could confess and get rid of it. Without either the concept of sin or the nomenclature, we live in an inexplicable, hovering gloom, or a skittering anxiety as we eat the poisonous berries of guilt and wonder why we have indigestion.

Our cultural abandonment of sin is a direct response to strains of American Puritanism, still festering in pockets into the twenty-first century. The Puritans got many things correct, including the right to religious freedom; however, their view of sin as stranglehold, sin as the focus of life, and sin as obsession, swung the religious pendulum far to the side of religious punishment—hellfire and damnation—forgetting about the far mightier power of God's love. The natural reaction to extremes is usually not, unfortunately, moderation, but a lunge to the opposite extreme, a sin-free consciousness that can't understand why happiness is still elusive.

As we've discussed, deep in the human psyche is the control room. Whoever controls this central place also controls the lighting. And lighting varies: thrills are likely to produce a Las Vegas neon effect; quiet contemplation resembles soft candlelight; everyday light for everyday things; darkness when we are lost; and for sin—woo-hoo!—in this room of our inner lives, sin is the big mirrored dance ball, twirling enticingly and casting bits of rainbow lights across every move we make. With our own reflection mirrored in a hundred facets, this ball hangs in the center.

Television crime shows (like *Criminal Minds*) portray a certain type of bad guy who looks like a nice man or woman on the outside—the Ted Bundy type, handsome, friendly. But the inside? Their actions—torture, rape, murder—reveal that their inner lives are lit by a brilliant disco ball spinning out of control and flinging the colors of death into the lives of the people they encounter.

Serial killers, sociopaths, and psychopaths are our culture's worst-case scenarios. They are not nice. They represent the human race at its worst; heaven help us all when they attain power. And many of them do.

At some point growing up, we all become aware of our inner room versus our outward persona—and the potential (for better or for worse) for spiritual schizophrenia. This inner room is home base for our lives, the place where we play flashbacks, dance, flirt, socialize, dream. The place where we collect and replay memories (pleasant or terrifying), on the walls of the mind's projector, the place where we live. Sometimes it takes a novelist to point out a big truth: "One's real life is almost always the life one doesn't lead."

Early on, I realized my persona looked like a painted doll in a crinoline petticoat, with an occasional skinned knee. But the inside. By the time I was twenty-five and had bottomed out, not only did the inner place look like a prison cell, the corners stuffed with the trash of my failed attempts at life, but the large disco dance ball hung incongruously over the disaster area, mirroring me and my failures off every wall in Technicolor rainbows.

Something was wrong in the center. I could no longer say I had never sinned. I was no longer nice.

That moment was the best thing that ever happened to me.

Okay, let's don't call it sin. Without using such an unattractive and overloaded word, there are other more politically correct, socially acceptable terms to describe behavior that doesn't measure up to our greatest potential. The most common word for sin in Greek is *hamartia,* which means "missing the mark." Picture a row of archers with targets fifty yards away, and one hits the bull's eye, but the rest glance the outer rings, and some overshoot altogether.

"Missing the mark" sounds so much more benign than "sin." After all, we're only human. And if we don't reach the goal of being nice or good all the time, well, who can be perfect? Nobody. The notion of missing the mark also carries with it an effort. We see the target; we see what needs to be done and we try, but our aim is poor and we don't accomplish what we set out to.

I personally prefer "missing the mark" to *parakoe*—flat out disobedience, sin on purpose.

Then there's *hettema,* which loosely translated means "fault." In geology, a fault refers to cracks in the earth's surface created from plates of rocks shifting in the earth's crust, causing fissures, crevices, and earthquakes. In terms of human character, a fault refers to a flaw or a defect. The concept of a fault plays out in two ways, the first having to do with a problem in our psychological construction that causes us to act out.

Literature teems with character flaws—a defect, a blind spot, an excess that causes the character's undoing. In the hierarchy of faults, pride is the biggest, baddest, meanest, because the character—take Oedipus, for example—doesn't see himself as he really is. Oedipus thinks he's going to save his city-state from famine and plague by finding the person responsible for killing the king. He has no clue that HE is the one, of course, who has killed the king, his own father, and married his mother. HE is the cause of his country's plague.

Robert Burns wrote a poem entitled, "To a Louse," in which he is sitting at church watching lice creep up the neck of an arrogant, snooty woman in front of him. She is oblivious to the insects and reigns like a queen in the pew. "Oh, would the Lord the giftie give us," says Burns, "to see ourselves as others see us."

Frankly, I'm not sure I could take it if I saw myself as others see me, which is why the second definition of *fault* is such a handy and popular method of escaping the truth about ourselves. Fault is also the cause of a disaster, as in "It's your fault we lost the baseball game. You struck out in the last inning with the bases loaded."

Pointing the finger is so deeply satisfying. We load our disappointment and outrage on the donkey of someone else's egregious mistake. We do not want to be reminded that WE struck out in the second inning or that it takes a whole team to win or lose a game; or that every member of the human race (including us) has at one time or another caused pain to another member of the human race through, yes, a character fault.

In exploring other facets of the glittering silver orb, the obvious observation is that the ball is covered with mirrors. "Me," "me," "me" is reflected a hundred times in tiny little squares. I'm not going into the doctrine of original sin, but Augustine's observation of a squalling, angry baby leaps to mind. These precious, little creatures may be adorable, but they're ruthless in their desire to get their needs met. What starts out as a survival mechanism, turns into pathology if the baby doesn't learn that he or she isn't the only person in the world—that other people exist outside the sphere of themselves, and some of them, (the nerve!) actually grow up to think *they* are at the center of the universe.

Paraptoma, or an unintentional slip, is a handy Greek word for another facet of acting destructively. Like it or not, blind spots come with the human package. Driving along the interstate, when you've checked both mirrors to pass a slow vehicle—a car materializes out of nowhere, just as you've crept into the left lane. We didn't see it coming. One of my blind spots cost $900, and I considered myself lucky.

Paraptoma also occurs when we feast on our foot, up to the ankle. Many years ago, when I was a student at Oxford, I told a young man at a garden party that the worst, most boring textbook I'd ever read was written by a man with his (fairly unusual) last name. The author, naturally, was the young man's uncle.

A related phenomenon is *agnoeema,* translated "ignorant when one should have known better." As the cuffs are being slapped on, we say, "But officer, I didn't know that the bag the nice man handed me was filled with drugs."

Or, from the crime shows on television, "I didn't mean to kill her. I just wanted to teach her a lesson."

Ignorance of the law, as they say, is no excuse.

My life has been a series of learning experiences, and in second grade, the growth curve was especially high. My friends and I learned that it was cheating to compare answers with each other. We thought we'd come up with a great system to get a higher grade. Cheating! At that moment we all lost a little of the sheen on our self images. But I didn't know... I didn't know... I didn't know....

Parabasis (besides the point in a Greek play when the chorus addresses the audience) means to cross a line intentionally. I'd prefer to think of myself as the innocent little second grader, ignorant of the rules, but in fact, I have crossed the line on purpose on occasion. I was reminded of this recently with a speeding ticket.

The law is a series of lines. Crossing them (and getting caught) results in a repercussion, from enforced driving school to capital punishment, depending on the severity of the crime. Unfortunately, the moral realm is a little less defined, both in terms of lines in the sand as well as in the consequences, even if you don't get caught.

Making unkind remarks about people results ultimately in isolation.

Calling "in" balls "out" too often means nobody wants to play tennis with you.

Every cruel gesture, every bitter word, every grudge, every lustful thought eventually wears us down on the inside. We become a container filled with acid, corroding from within. Nobody else may know, but our little room of the soul becomes barely habitable.

Elizabeth Vining writes about John Donne, naming different facets of the glimmering, glowing ball of self and sin:

> John Donne preached as one who knew by experience the slipperiness of habitual sin; the merry sins; the laughing sins that become crying sins; the whispering sins that we rock in our hearts, tossing and tumbling them in our imaginations; the forgotten sins; the unconsidered, unconfessed, unrepentant sins and all the sins that we call small: enough lascivious glances to make up an adultery, enough covetous wishes for a robbery, enough angry words for a murder.

The study of sin is called "hamartiology," and it's fascinating to examine why we do the things we know we shouldn't and why we don't do the things we know we should.

Sin is captivating, first by being juicy, luscious, and immediately satisfying. The sinful choice is almost always more interesting than Doing the Right Thing. Just ask the first pair of humans. They had it all. Succulent fruit dropped off the trees in the garden of Eden, right into their hands. The perfect climate meant they didn't have to wear clothes, and their nudity revealed two perfect bodies made for each other's enjoyment. An added bonus was their control over all the animals in Paradise.

It was an idyllic life, the kind of experience we aim for on cruise vacations. But no. Adam and Eve wanted the only thing God told them they couldn't have.

Dante said it took six hours for Adam and Eve to get restless and whiny. "Why can't we have THAT fruit? It's not fair. What good is Paradise if we can't have the one thing we want?"

Personally, I think Dante was optimistic in thinking Adam and Eve held out for a whole six hours, but then again, I'm a citizen of a country where one of the deepest credos is instant gratification.

The second reason sin is captivating is that it is captivating—it holds you captive. If I do that thing I know isn't right, then it has power over me. I may be dancing a jig under the mirrored ball, but somewhere in the corner of the room I call my soul, I know I have sold out. The more I sell my better self out, the worse I feel, even though I may not be able to put my finger on the problem.

The word *civilized* conjures images of tea parties, intellectual discussions, peace talks, nonprofits working for the benefit of the less fortunate—in other words, people being polite, kind, and unselfish. We learned in tenth grade that civilization started in the fertile crescent of the Tigris and Euphrates Rivers. Knowing that civilized behavior is the goal of any enlightened society, one wouldn't suspect that the history of civilization is shot through with demolition, devastation, annihilation, ruin, rape, pillage, and death.

And so it goes. The history of the world is an account of violence; the invention of farm implements, art, culture, writing, science, religion, communication, and advances in medicine, technology, and machinery can't keep up with the swords, gunpowder, tanks, bombers, and nuclear missiles the best and brightest of the human race have devised to contribute to the planet's demise.

Whether we are like sheep who nibble ourselves out of the pasture, down the ravine, and into a dark chasm, lost, where we lie down and die or whether we fall as a herd off the cliff, sin is the chief sheep killer on the earth.

Just because we don't currently have the barbarians swooping down on our mid-America cities with their maces, spears, and catapults of fire, it doesn't mean that they won't. Only now with advanced warfare and the rise of individual acts of terrorism, we may never see it coming.

It appears there is something wrong with the human race, not just in individuals.

We can call the Thing-in-the-Center-that's-Not-Right "sin," or we can call it something else. But make no mistake, it's functioning quite well, unfortunately.

The problem is how to deal with it.

9

A Trip to the Beach After Ten Feet of Snow

Forgiveness is the fragrance that the violet sheds
on the heel that has crushed it.
—Mark Twain

UNFORTUNATELY, HUMAN BEINGS tend to foul our own nests. Fortunately, news is that we don't have to sit in the squalor.

The advantage of calling sin "sin" is that we have a handle on what we're dealing with. The church made a killing off of sin in the Middle Ages with indulgences and other ways to make reparation for wrong-doing, because even the illiterate peasants knew when they'd erred and strayed from God's ways. Though the system swelled the coffers of the institution, the church's structure for penitence still worked for purging the feelings of guilt and for cleaning up the little room of the soul.

In a nutshell, the system goes like this. God created human beings as good. He gave us the choice of staying good and enjoying Paradise, or else rebelling.

From the first succulent bite, awareness of good and evil hit us over the head, sort of like a large cast iron skillet. Our first parents realized, oops, we are not God. We didn't create ourselves. We didn't make the rules... we only broke them.

How on earth could these two puny human beings make things right again? They couldn't. God had to take the initiative once again. After watching us kill and hate each other for millennia, God finally said, "They're never going to figure it out on their own, so I guess I'll have to go down there and help them."

So He did. But He had to show up looking like the rest of us so we could hear Him and not run away in stark terror.

In the Sermon on the Mount, Jesus sat among the rocks and gave out new interpretations of the old rules. (Not only don't murder, don't get angry, for example. Some tough stuff—all of which was good advice, but not enough to pay back the debt we owed for trying to be as smart as God in the first place.) To even the cosmic score, Jesus let sin kill Him on the cross. He died from all the hate, the jealousy, the betrayal, the "hand washing" of the people around Him.

What killed Jesus was not some grand and glorious warfare or subterfuge. No, the religious leaders didn't like Him because they didn't want to give up their prestigious positions in the community; His disciple Judas went behind His back to betray Him; Pontius Pilate gave in because he didn't want a riot during Passover.

Basically, one reason I'm a Christian is because I got tired of sitting in my own garbage. Forgiveness is a magnificent thing.

So, the sin of the human race, played out through specific historical people, killed God. And it wasn't a nuclear war. It was the small stuff, the seedy decisions we all make at one time or another.

Fortunately, that's not the end of the story. Jesus' death on the cross conquered sin, but that alone would have been a draw, the score tied. Even Steven.

Jesus also conquered death. Easter happened. Jesus didn't stay dead, and because He rose from the dead, so can we.

The early church understood the process well. The sins that killed God are the same ugly behaviors we still inflict on each other. But we're not stuck with filling our little room with the trash and refuse of our guilt. When we recognize our sin, feel sorry for being the jerks (and worse) that we can be, we can ask forgiveness, and God will clean our house for us.

It took me fifty-six years to see it was my own sin, anger, and envy that led to the biting incident with my sister. A nicer, better sister would have thought, "How great that she gets to stay for another movie." But no. I was furious. Then I provoked a fight. Then I got revenge. And finally, I held on to my self-righteousness for decades. When my sister and God both forgave me, it felt like a trip to the beach after living in ten feet of snow.

Basically, one reason I'm a Christian is because I got tired of sitting in my own garbage. Forgiveness is a magnificent thing.

We see "Jesus Saves!" written on billboards, carved into the side of mountains along the highway, printed on pamphlets handed out by the Salvation Army. We think, what kind of religious fanatic would take the time to spray paint "Jesus Saves!" on an overpass? What, exactly, does Jesus save?

He saves us from ourselves.

10

Begging, Basking, Chatting, Screaming, and Silence

Prayer is the soul's sincerest desire,
Uttered or unexpressed.
—James Montgomery

MY BABY GRANDSON, CARTER, has only five words in his vocabulary, but he manages to communicate clearly. He toddles over with a grin, raises his arms, and wiggles pudgy little fingers at Papa Dad and me. We know exactly what he wants (and who can resist picking him up?).

It takes going through a different developmental stage for tiny tykes to realize that grown-ups aren't omniscient. Babies have communicated with signals and telepathy for months, and Mom and Dad and Sister understood perfectly—well, most of the time. Yet, at some point, we all have to start working at communication.

I know I shouldn't put this chapter's bottom line here on the first page, but the thing about prayer is that God doesn't really care about the words; He wants a dialogue with our central heart-spirit-place, the control center, the soul; and conversation takes as many forms as there are people.

Circumstances come and go. Minds give way. Bodies deteriorate and die. Soul talk (which may not involve words at all) is what lasts for eternity. Our time on earth gives us practice in communicating with God.

I used to worry about prayer. What do I say? It was bad enough to say something stupid in the classroom, but in front of God? The Lord's Prayer was okay, but who at age nine understands what "trespasses" are?

And what did the Lord's Prayer have to do with my friends and me? Over the years, it became rote, calcified instead of growing like living tissue, as the bones of our body grow, expanding to reach a mature height and understanding.

After my liquor cabinet conversion, my father gave me brochures on how to pray. He must have heard me sprinting right in and asking God for what I wanted first. To solve my abysmal selfishness, he gave me a brochure on the ACTS prayer: Adoration, Confession, Thanksgiving, Supplication (asking first for others' needs, then our own).

The problem with a prayer formula is that, though it works well for people whose minds are more organized than mine, my prayer time ends up all over the map, and I can't stick to the formula. When, indeed, I manage to concentrate hard enough and get through to the end, the only feeling I have is one of accomplishment, not communication. And love is not part of the task; I feel neither God's love for me nor my love for Him. But, by golly, I've said my daily prayer.

Books have been written on different prayer styles for different personalities, which reduces the guilt at not praying up to par according to the experts' format. Whew—if God made each of us special, then our conversation with Him is going to reflect that.

Most of this chapter is about personal prayer, but public prayer—though banned by the courts—is also important. I live in a Texas town small enough that the city council always opens with a prayer. No one's bombed us yet or arrested our mayor. And, as I tell my students, prayer's not really banned from any place, including school or football games. By banning Christian prayer from being said aloud, we are banning only *audible* prayer, including prayer that Christians may not condone—prayers to all kinds of non-Christian gods, voodoo, sticking pins in effigies, Satanic prayers, or rain dances (which I'm not against in our drought-ridden part of the country, but not very suitable in grade school classrooms). Nobody says you can't pray silently.

Also, intercessory prayer for total strangers is important—for the people that fire engines and ambulances are racing to, for people on the nightly news. Pray unceasingly, with or without words.

Anyone who's ever been the "new kid" at a new school—especially in the jungles of junior high—remembers all those other cocky kids, ready to pounce, bully, laugh at—or ignore—the fresh meat. New kids stand with a tray at the side of the lunchroom, thinking, how can I possibly find a friend among all these smarter, better-looking, more self-assured adolescents?

Oh, the agony of a shy, mumbling twelve-year-old. Making a friend requires conversation. Growing and maintaining a friendship also requires conversation, which is precisely the problem. Conversation means knowing when to talk and when to listen. When to initiate and when to back off. When to give in and when to stand firm. When to ask and when to accept. When to apologize and when to accept an apology.

Prayer is really just conversation, but some of us feel like adolescents when it comes to talking to God. How do you make friends with God? Same way as in junior high—by talking to Him about your life. Nothing is off-limits or trivial or silly.

Children pray to get good Christmas presents. Adolescents pray that they'll be popular. College students pray to pass a class. Young adults pray to find a job, a life mate, a nice apartment. Middle-aged people pray for their children. Elderly people pray for an easy death.

Prayer is how we get to know God, like making a friend. With one big difference. Because God is the other person involved, you can always count on His end of the bargain. Friends, on the other hand, fall from pedestals; do stupid, hurtful things; forget important events; can't come at the last minute. But not God.

If we keep the conversation going, we understand, sooner or later, that His No is almost always a better thing. Oh, yeah—when I didn't get the job I prayed for, I got a better one. Oh, yeah—my former fiancé turned out to have a secret drug habit and is now in prison. Oh, yeah—if I hadn't gone through that misery, I wouldn't have learned the lesson that has made me so happy now. When life is rotten, watch for the redemption. Watch for it because if God's in the central control room, He can see farther than we can.

God has the airplane view and not the ground view; He can see what's coming over the hill when we can't see past our hut. One of my favorite prayers from the Episcopal prayer book says, paraphrased, "Bless us, O Lord, with those things which we don't deserve and are too ignorant to ask for."

The fact is, God is waiting with a sack bigger than Santa's, filled with blessings. Sometimes, He leaves surprise blessings on the kitchen table, and we don't have to ask. But most often, conversation is important—asking for what we need. As the old cliché goes, sometimes God says, Yes, in response; sometimes He says, No or Later. The point is to keep asking.

A Christian man asked God for a bigger house, the kind of home his wealthy parents raised him in. He felt inferior in his small house. He wanted to give his children the same luxury he had growing up. All his friends and relatives had bigger houses. His children had to share a room. So he prayed. Year in and year out for several years, he prayed for a bigger house. If anything, his finances grew tighter.

After a couple of years of this conversation, the man began to sense that God was speaking back. God was telling him that getting a bigger house wouldn't make anything better. God reminded the man of how much he loved his wife, how happy his kids were, how healthy they were, how the family had enough money to go on vacations and to buy their children what they needed. The big house, the man realized, represented status, keeping up with the Joneses, and, in the deepest sense, trying to impress a cold, unloving father—all things that weren't essential to true happiness.

The man's conversation with God changed. "Hey—look at all the blessings You've given me! I don't need that house. Thank You for my happy life." Sappy, maybe, but an important truth. (Pollyanna wasn't all wrong.) And rehearsing over and over what God has done for us is a good way to remember that prayer is a two-way radio, not something we broadcast over the airwaves with no receiver.

In some cultures, begging is an honorable profession. Jesus

encouraged us to beg to God, not because God is withholding a blessing until we reach a certain point of holiness or deservedness, but because He knows what's best for us, and we're so often clueless.

We are children, begging for candy before supper and angry when the answer is No. God doesn't love us! What good is prayer anyway?

Sometimes it takes a lifetime to understand that we need to keep asking if what we want is important to us. If we listen to the response, God will explain why, eventually, that the answer is no, or else we will trade in the old desire with a request for something more nourishing.

Talking to God is important because it keeps the conversation going—and it reminds us to keep our eyes on the Giver, not the gift.

Ignorance is not bliss. Ignorance is panicking because you don't know where your children are at night. Ignorance is dangerous. Before going through every passage of life, we look ahead and think we know what's coming around the mountain driving six white horses—like the A-level high school student who thinks college English will be a breeze (not realizing that the college class is now filled with A-level students, and some of the former A students are going to be making the Cs).

Ignorance keeps us from not asking for the right things. But ignorance is just one way we thwart the blessing-fest that God has planned for us. We look around at our lives, see the bad things that afflict the human race (and us in particular), and doubt that God can redeem any of the mess we're in.

Fact: Everyone, in the hidden room inside, has burdens and regrets.

Fact: Most of us like to dress our shop windows with decorative pieces of ourselves, so people won't know what's going on in the inner room, where we really live. We fear nobody will understand us, nobody would like us if they did, and nobody has it as bad as we do.

Prayer is the cleaning service that comes in, dusts off the furniture of our lives, disinfects the floor, and carries the regrets to the trash, and all the while God is reminding us, "I love you. I understand you. I forgive you. I want the best for you because I made you just the way you are."

Every other summer our family rents a cabin at the YMCA of the Rockies in Estes Park and we hike in Rocky Mountain National Park, where the pines and spruce turn common oxygen into pungent whiffs of air, where streams ripple, and the rugged hulk of the Front Range becomes the backdrop for all activities. We've scampered and trudged on hundreds of hikes to picnic on the shores of glistening lakes, where ham sandwiches taste better than ham sandwiches at home.

My favorite analogy of life is like a hike, with a trailhead at Alberta Falls and an end point at Sky Pond. We traipse along, knowing we will not always have perfect weather. Certain aspects of the landscape, like a boulder field or an icy patch or a sheer cliff, make for rugged challenges.

The first step to a happy life is accepting this fact: life ain't easy. Sure, we reach small plateaus of bliss, but they don't last for many miles, and sure enough, here we are again, lost in the forest.

Prayer is the conversation along the way with the One who created us for the hike.

Eager to serve, a man had been praying for God to reveal His will for his life. What should he do? One morning, he woke up and found a giant boulder—taller than he was—in his front yard. He stared at the rock and heard a voice from heaven say, "I want you to push the boulder."

Grateful his prayer had been answered, the man changed into work clothes, rolled up his sleeves and began to push. Nothing happened. So he pushed again. The boulder wouldn't budge. And again and again and again he shoved with all his might against the rock.

Determined to do God's will, the man lay down on his back and pushed with his feet. The stone still refused to move. Going into the garage, he retrieved a long metal tool to use as a crowbar. Nothing. Getting tired, he went inside to gulp down a power drink, then resumed his task.

At the end of the day with no success, he stood in the shower, depressed. He had failed in the task that God had given him to do. Had he heard God wrong? He had used all his strength and now could barely stand up as the water washed over his exhausted body. He again heard a voice. "I asked you to push the rock, not to move it. Well done, good and faithful servant."

Oh.

God's ways are not our ways.

Obedience to God's will is more important than success in the world's, our parents', our friends', or our own terms.

When God answers our prayers, sometimes the response seems ludicrous and impossible.

Sometimes what God wants out of us is not the same as what we want out of ourselves.

His agenda often has nothing to do with a tangible result.

Then there's the silence of God, a frightening, frigid space like the walk-in freezer in our church kitchen, where rows of huge bags of frozen vegetables loom, and where, in spite of a rational mind, I experience a brief moment of alarm when I enter, fearing that I'll get trapped and die.

Dante's lowest rung of hell was an ice pit, where the miserable, godless people couldn't even cry because it was so cold their tears froze. Satan himself was stuck in the ice forever.

God's silence can seem like sitting in a tub of ice waiting for the sun to rise.

Why does God allow us to go through periods of silence, when our existence is hell, and His existence seems nonexistent? Having survived several stretches of frosty silence from the One I look to for guidance, peace, and redemption—none of which seemed to be forthcoming—I've discovered a few useful facts that, frankly, (although I know better) I wish I wouldn't ever have to use again.

Babies grow when they sleep. We grow when God is silent. God's silence is a cool-down period for our hot, flaming, undesirable passions. Fiery cravings (lust, success, and all the other luscious things we think we can't live without), our blazing determination to override a perfectly good plan for our lives, the conflagration of controlling the people around us. A period of time in the old freezer cools all desires except the desire for God.

God is God, and I am not.

I once heard a former prisoner of war speak of his solitary confinement and isolation in a cell for three years. He said, "The only person with me was God. Everyone should have the privilege of spending three years in isolation with God."

As long as there's life there's hope. God will eventually speak again. We will not freeze to death unless we choose to.

We can flap our lips all we want, but closing the mouth and listening into the silence is a good thing. Conversation is, after all, a two-way street. God often seems silent when He is telling us something we don't want to hear.

The medieval carnival was a time before Lent to make merry, a wild party with jugglers, games, masques, costumes, parades, wild antics, lots of drinking. The word *carnival* comes from the Latin root "carn" meaning "meat" and "vale" meaning "good-bye"—so since it was good-bye to meat for the next six weeks before Easter, the carnival was a raucous and ribald festival. Shrove Tuesday carnivals still take place all over the world today, especially in countries with a high Roman Catholic population.

Today's typical carnival refers to a Ferris wheel, stomach-churning rides, and booths that offer stuffed animals as prizes for, say, shooting ducks or tossing hoops. A traveling carnival in the parking lot of the mall is an annual field-force magnet for my grandchildren. Not to mention the cotton candy and funnel cakes.

Anyway, older adults have difficulty hearing at carnivals and other places like pinball arcades and crowded restaurants. Much of life these days seems to take place in locations with lots of background noise, like malls (yes, I am one of those older adults who has trouble hearing over rock bands, Muzak, and crowds).

The problem with having a conversation with God is that I have to get out of earshot of my iPad, my iPhone, my TV, and my radio. It's hard to hear God's whisper at a carnival.

Fifty years ago, teens across America put Mercurochrome in baby oil, slathered their bodies with it, and lay roasting on beaches, rooftops, and patios to get that bronzed, movie-star tan. These days, basking in the sun has become a hazardous enterprise, but I still remember the warmth seeping down into my bones and the delight of lying on a beach towel while listening to the waves with my friends in Port Aransas.

Basking in the love of God is another form of prayer. Coming from a product oriented family and inheriting more than my share of life goals that measured success in terms of social or career accomplishments, I was not a basker in life. I was a doer, go, go, go. During my children's teenage years, when my son had carved a four-inch, royal blue Mohawk from his thick, beautiful hair and set it up with Elmer's glue, and my daughter had gone to a new school where the girls were mean as only catty female teens can be, I felt depressed because these things were only the tip of the iceberg concerning that period of our lives.

My prayer life was silent, and my soul felt gritty from walking through this particular desert. My neighbor said, "Why don't you just sit and bask in God's love for ten minutes every morning?"

God loved me? I found the evidence lacking. That was the first issue.

Then, basking? How, exactly, did one bask in God's love? Determined to try anything, I climbed into my most comfortable chair and announced to God that I would be sitting there for ten minutes just waiting for His rays of love to warm my skin and give me a spiritual tan.

I have to say, it took awhile, days and weeks of sitting in the chair until the chair broke and we had to replace it. But I learned how to bask in the love of God.

What helped in this spiritual discipline was an understanding of athletic training, a good metaphor for spiritual growth. Football, tennis, track, baseball, swimming, and even, I suppose, sports like curling—pushing your body until it hurts. Running one more lap than you think you can. Drilling the same play, over and over and over and over. As my husband said once in a sermon, Jesus doesn't want admirers; he wants disciples, which means discipline, which means practicing the faith, which means trying, failing, getting up again, for the rest of our lives, until we fall exhausted but at peace into the feather bed of heavenly rest.

Becoming a spiritual warrior takes going through spiritual boot camp. The battle is against our own clouds of doubt, fear, or inertia that form a chilly barrier and hide the love of God. What's hard to remember is that the sun shines above the atmosphere no matter what, ready to break through and warm us to the bone.

I had a friend and colleague who was a Vietnam vet. When I'd ask him how his day was going, even on a bad day he'd grin and say, "Hey, life's good. Nobody's shooting at me."

In *Matterhorn,* a novel about the Vietnam War, Lieutenant Mellas led his men in an attack not likely to succeed, an assault ordered by a colonel eager to be a general—and making decisions far away from the realities of combat. In a lull during the fighting, Mellas surveyed the carnage of his men's bodies, and the terrier of fear shook him. "Stripped to a scream, undressed to a cry of pain, he sobbed his anger at God in hoarse words that hurt his throat. He asked for nothing now, nor did he wonder if he'd been bad or good."

Life in the foxhole had become a savage joke God had played on him. He cursed God, and "in that cursing Mellas for the first time really talked with his God. Then he cried, tears and snot mixing together as they streamed down his face." He realized that his cries "were the rage and hurt of a newborn child, at last, however roughly, being taken from the womb."

Mellas's prayer, such as it was, was a birth into the kind of courage it took for him to become a hero and save his men, which he did in the next sally against the Vietcong.

Though hard for us to understand at the time and surrounded by the bloody butchery of our personal battles, God is on call, listening to the scream of anger, the heart-cry of life-anguish—"on call" like an obstetrician, ready to help us give birth to the brave new person we will be born into.

Seminars on "success" promote the idea of positive self-talk. We are in constant communication with ourselves, driving down the road, in a meeting, washing the dishes; and apparently a critically high percentage of our self-talk is negative (some say over 70 percent): Why did you make that stupid remark? Your mother was right; you'll never amount to anything. Most people you work with don't like you.

One of my friends said that a way to stop the negative self-talk is to pray. Ask God for more positive thoughts. After all, when we talk to God, we can overhear the conversation ourselves, and it's bound to be more constructive than the continual chipping away we humans do to our own self-esteem.

Historically, the medieval church prayed in Latin. The people didn't understand Latin. The notion of making up prayers on your own had yet to come into its own, although people like Teresa of Avila prayed with passion, and not from the Book of Hours. Or in Latin.

I come from a tradition that recites prayers written over five hundred years ago, some going back even farther. Some churches feel stifled by old prayers written by someone else—even though the prayers are updated from time to time. Praying from a prayer book is like walking the same path or jogging down the same streets in a routine. But by paying attention, new things always leap to the conscious mind.

On the other hand, extemporaneous prayers offer spontaneity, a freshness of thought. Group prayer ties the prayees together in a special bond. Most hymns are prayers in song. The point is, it doesn't matter how we pray.

Whether we know it or not, God is listening to us, even if we don't use any words at all, even if it seems that He doesn't answer our requests. In the Bible, Paul prayed for God to remove a thorn from his side. God said No, and Paul apparently died with the thorn or issue unresolved.

Did Paul quit praying? No. God always has reasons for the way He answers prayers, and I believe we will understand the reasons as soon as we pass from this world into the next.

11

The Thought of Dying Makes Me Nervous

The sense of death is most in apprehension.
—Shakespeare

LET'S FACE IT, THE NOTION OF HELL—though less comforting—is more intriguing than the notion of heaven. Literature anthologies include Dante's *Inferno* in all its bloody, macabre, repulsive totality, with barely a nod to *Paradise*'s gentle, increasing light.

In fact, the question good Christians are afraid to ask is, "Will heaven be boring?" Which in turn hides the deeper and more frightening questions: "Does heaven really exist?" and "Will I get to go there?"

By the time we're sixty, most of us have had a ringside seat to observe the end of life, watching friends and loved ones pass away before our eyes. We are helpless to stop the onslaught of slow and creeping death, abrupt death, accidental death, and the myriad other deaths that plague and terrify the human race.

By the time we're sixty, we also realize that life is as fragile as a Styrofoam cup in a windstorm. And we know it will end. So we joke about death and taxes as being the only sure things in life.

My daughter, Caroline, had a special relationship with her grandfather, Jerre, until he died when she was three years old. Months before his death, he was wheelchair-bound with tubes in his nose attached to a canister of oxygen. Every time we visited, Caroline would run through the house, gleefully shouting, "Jerre!" when she spied him, then climb into his lap and snuggle.

Before the visitation at the funeral home, we talked with Caroline about death and dying, preparing her the best we could. The minute she walked into the room, she saw him. "There's Jerre!" she said and ran up to the casket. I followed closely behind. She stopped. She peered over the rim of the casket. She turned to me and said, "Mommy, Jerre looks scary."

I sat down with her on my lap and again went over heaven, life after death, and how much Jerre loved her. She understood a little more, this time with the visualization of what it looks like to be dead. She was no longer scared.

Death is the central existential trauma for human beings, but death is scariest when it hits home like a bomb in a pickle barrel. Death is not just for other people.

As my father was dying, he said, "I know all about death and heaven. But this is different. It's *my* death we're talking about here." The threat of immediate extinction brings into sharp focus those hazy generalities we've managed to avoid.

"It's *my* death we're talking about here," when the grim reaper knocks on *my* door. Wallace Stevens wrote anti-Christian poetry, yet apparently made a deathbed conversion when he looked into death's big black eyes and glimpsed the empty back of beyond.

Dying is the one thing every human being on earth has in common with every other human being. And, yes, it's *my* death we're talking about here. And yours.

The church in the Middle Ages got a lot of things wrong, but they understood one thing more clearly than we do. Life was short and hard-scrabble difficult. The afterlife loomed above them, closer than storm clouds heavy with rain, breathing blustery fear into daily life. Medieval literature is saturated with dying and with the afterlife—either heaven, purgatory, or hell.

Just as no one can explain to a fetus what the world will be like, so no one can explain to a human what an afterlife will be like.

The Renaissance shifted attention from the afterlife to this life, focusing on human achievement here and now, and pushing the specter of death toward the back of the stage, like a backdrop of painted clouds instead of the real thing. Concern with the afterlife was no longer the focus of day-to-day performance.

These days, death seems as far away as the moon. We know it circles our lives above us, but we try not to think about it. Death is the thing to be cheated by chemotherapy, good eating habits, exercise, and other sound and healthy choices. Most of us don't have to look death in the face until we reach twice the life expectancy of a thousand years ago. If we take care of ourselves, and if good luck and genetics hold, we get a two for one special in terms of back-to-back life spans.

Sooner or later, though, we answer the doorbell, and guess who's there—the fellow with the scythe and black hood. And we come to the moment of truth, the threshold that all of life has prepared us for—every word we've spoken, every relationship we've had, every decision we've made. Now! The show is over.

American TV, movies, books, and Internet thrive on preparing us how NOT to meet death, thrusting pop-ups of nutritious diets and exercise programs in our faces, flashing information on how to stay alive come (as they say) hell or high water. But who teaches us how to die? Hospice comes in at the end, but what about the years before the diagnosis? Who teaches us that death can be a splendid crossover event?

In fact, who teaches us how to live? Our culture is focused on maintaining perfect, wrinkle-free skin and a slim, well-toned body dressed in stylish clothes. What about real life? What about real death?

Three years ago, a tumor the size of a large gumball infarcted at the base of my brain, dead center in my head. In excruciating pain, I said goodbye to my family, then sat in the passenger seat while my husband flew down Interstate 10 to the Neurological ICU in San Antonio. Methodically, I went through my journal, checking for stupid, idiotic, or silly remarks because I didn't know if that night would be my last. I wanted anyone reading the journal after I died to think I was smarter and nicer than I really am.

As it turned out, surgery removed the tumor; it also provided me new eyes to see life and a new joyful spirit, belting from within like an opera star. Nothing—not chores, not art, not writing, not my relationships with family and friends—has been the same since.

I got a second chance to do it right and to think about how to live, what it means to love my family, and God—and what's in store for us after we're embalmed or burned. I ditched the old baggage and started packing for a new trip, stuffing all the joy, family, friends, love, peace, and fun I could in my daily suitcase. You never know when death's taxi service will ring the bell, and when it does, I'll be ready. Or at least more ready than I was.

Near-death stories are a dime a dozen, and most involve a view of one's body in a hospital bed from ceiling level, and a bright, welcoming light, along with a soothing, balmy peace. However, many years ago, I heard about a near-death story of an older woman, selfish and spiteful, who experienced only deep, penetrating blackness and prickles and stabs of fear. When she came to, she knew instantly that she needed to turn her life around because living forever in such dark misery would be...well, hell. I don't remember where this story came from, but I remember the courage it must have taken for the woman to tell her story as a warning to other unforgiving, mean-spirited people who don't think earthly behavior has unearthly consequences.

The assortment of religious afterlife theology offers many delicious and heavenly courses to finish off life's meal. Atheism provides nothingness, which may sound good on a frenzied, chaotic day, but doesn't offer much in terms of comfort or pleasant expectation. Atheism also zeroes in on this life, as if that's all there is—which leads to dependence on fickle, deadly, or coincidental fate for happiness.

Human beings emerge into the world with a yearning for more life after it ends. Yet, just as no one can explain to a fetus what the world will be like, so no one can explain to a human what an afterlife will be like. We know where Uncle Clyde's body, warts and all, is planted, and we leave flowers next to the cold, etched granite tombstone: 1934–2014. But we hope against hope that Uncle Clyde lives on somewhere, somehow in a better place; and we hope that we will, too.

Sixty years ago, five and dime stores sold a fist-size ball in which tiny figures and trinkets had been wrapped tightly at intervals in a yarn-like skein with strips of crepe paper. I still recall the thrill of unwinding the paper to find baubles along the way and to reach the center where a larger toy waited discovery.

As we get closer to our own center, and the endgame draws near, we hope, hope, hope to find a treasure instead of nothing.

Besides an innate desire to live on after the body decomposes, humans seem to need an afterlife that somehow, if only metaphorically, resembles what we know on earth. The ancient Egyptian kings believed that they could take it with them, loading up their spectacular tombs with all the gold and treasures they could pack into the musty inner cavity of the pyramids when they entered the afterlife. (Several millennia later, the jewels and riches went into museums or the pockets of wealthy bandits disguised as collectors, archeologists, or investors.)

I'm a Christian because in Christ, I know where home is, and I've been promised that I'm going there.

As a result of plundering these death caches, we realize that the chances are good that the afterlife takes place on a different plane of existence from the atomic/cellular makeup of gold, silver, and rubies, or physical bodies. The stuff of earth doesn't travel well. A nonmaterial afterlife is more conceivable, an eternity spent without the broken legs, arthritis, and other pain our bodies inflict on us—a spiritual place, which is what most religions offer.

Besides longing for life to continue after we die and our desire for a spiritual hereafter free from bodily pain, the human race also seems to need an afterlife that rewards good behavior or punishes wickedness committed during the duration of our three score and ten here on earth.

It doesn't take a genius to figure out that life isn't fair. The righteous are downtrodden; the evil prosper. And it's been this way since the beginning. The need to believe in divine justice in the face of such gross inequity seems to be built into the consciousness of ethical, rational, good-seeking people. The Greeks' religion offered the promise of Elysium for the righteous, the heroic, the gods and their relatives; Hades for the run-of-the-mill citizen; and Tartarus, a dungeon of torment for the wicked.

Muslims believe that life on earth is a test, filled with deeds and actions that will influence where you end up forever—Jannah on the one hand for good deeds or Jaharnan for the depraved or immoral. Buddhism and Hinduism share a similarity in their views of the afterlife, with progressive levels of reincarnation until the soul reaches the sublime state of Nirvana (the end of craving, suffering, ignorance, greed, hate, delusion). No self is independent of the universe and one can travel up or down the scale, depending on behavior in the only span of life we are conscious of—now, on earth.

I can go on and on about the intricacies of the afterlife theology of the Latter Day Saints, Jehovah's Witnesses, and Seventh Day Adventists, but the theology I'm interested in here is orthodox Christianity, and what it offers to believers about the possibility of life after this life.

The fact is that no matter how much we want to know what happens after we die, speculation is like hearing rumors of Antarctica before explorers had actually been there and returned. We have reports of near-death experiences, we have the creative imaginations of people like Dante, and we have historical accounts of eyewitnesses who saw what happened after Jesus died and rose from the dead on Easter.

Jesus did not look like a zombie.

He did not look like a ghost.

His body was recognizable, and it is this phenomenon, this visual change in the life energy of a human being that Christians hang their hat on, along with the promise that we, too, will transform into resurrected bodies when the time comes. After His resurrection, Jesus exuded a life energy, disseminated like an aura. This is not superstition; it's a description from written accounts of what His resurrected body looked like.

Because one of the laws of physics is that energy on the earth cannot be created or destroyed but only transformed, the life energy of our centers, our "souls" will be changed drastically but will still be recognizable. We will no longer lug our tiresome and exhausted bodies around with us, but we'll be able to communicate and move and have our being in another plane of existence.

We will receive all the love we've ever needed; we will understand the mysteries that have haunted us; we will be washed clean in the parts of ourselves we don't know exist; we will see the face of God.

The vision I received of heaven when I almost died with the infarcted tumor was a place where, even though the pain of the tumor was ten times that of a brain freeze—the joy I experienced was one hundred times more intense and pure than I've ever felt in this life, ever.

I'm a Christian because in Christ, I know where home is, and I've been promised that I'm going there.

The exhibit Bodies tripped a wire somewhere deep in my consciousness, besides creating a symphony of goose bumps as I walked from case to case, where scientists had stripped off the layers of the human body to reveal each separate system: the nervous system, the circulatory system, the reproductive, digestive, muscular, skeletal systems. In each display stood a former real live person, stripped of everything except one working system.

Even with all the brainiacs in the world working on figuring out how cells relate, examining subatomic particles of life, existence is a mystery.

What kick-started our universe is a mystery.

Getting up in the morning—coordinating eyes, ears, legs, mouth, bladder, stomach—is a mystery.

When all is said and done, we are stardust. Animated chemicals with consciousness of our existence. With choices we can make and choices made for us.

Recently, I splattered paint on my arm by accident. Looking down at the familiar appendage, I wondered once again how my arm came to be my arm. Some things, I thought to myself, I'll never understand.

As long as my brain doesn't develop lesions or suffer from a burst blood vessel, the choices available for shaping my reality have to do with rearranging the furniture of my life and learning to live with limitations.

God is God. I am not. The universe is laced with an energy more powerful than electricity, than the atomic bomb: love. And God is love.

No, I have not worked through all the struggles in my life. But I've suffered enough to know that there's another side past the wall of fire, and a hand that reaches through the flames to draw me close.

Bottom line: I am a Christian because I choose to believe that God loves me, forgives me, died for me, and will give me life forever. I will join Job, who said, "Though He slay me, yet will I trust him."

For Further Reading

THE FIRST THING I WOULD recommend is the Bible. Not only is it the world's greatest all-time best seller, but it's a guide for life, for every possible circumstance, problem, or thorny question in, yes, even the twenty-first century, a millennium or two after it first came out. Not only that, reading the Bible brings the reader closer to the author of all life.

When I gathered all my information for a bibliography, I realized I had, literally, thousands of good books to recommend. Depending on how scholarly or how unscholarly you want to be, you can scope out some of the following suggestions and, I hope, find what you're looking for. The following is a limited and subjective list of recent books that may lead you to other books:

Beckwith, Francis J., William Lane Craig and J.P. Moreland, eds. *To Everyone an Answer: A Case for the Christian Worldview.* Downers Grove, IL: InterVarsity Press, 2004.

Bush, L. Russ. *Classical Readings in Christian Apologetics: A.D. 100–1800.* Grand Rapids, MI: Zondervan, 1983.

Beilby, James. T*hinking about Christian Apologetics: What It Is and Why We Do It.* Downers Grove, IL: InterVarsity Press, 2011.

Dulles, Avery. *A History of Apologetics.* San Francisco: Ignatius, 2005.

Engberg, Jakob. Anders-Christian Jacobsen, Anders-Christian and Jörg Ulrich, eds. I*n Defence of Christianity: Early Christian Apologists.* Vol. 14. Frankfurt am Main: Peter Lang Edition, 2014.

Geisler, Norman. *Baker Encyclopedia of Christian Apologetics.* Grand Rapids, MI: Baker, 1999.

Kreeft, Peter, and Ronald K. Tacelli. *Pocket Handbook of Christian Apologetics.* Downers Grove, IL: InterVarsity Press, 2003. (Condensed from their more expansive *Handbook,* 1994).

Sproul, R. C. *Defending Your Faith: An Introduction to Apologetics.* Wheaton, IL: Crossway, 2003.

Stott, John. *Basic Christianity.* Grand Rapids, MI: Wm. B. Eerdmans, 1959.

Taylor, James. *Introducing Apologetics.* Grand Rapids, MI: Baker Academic, 2013.

Authors who have written multiple excellent books in the field of apologetics include the following:

Diogenes Allen
C. S. Lewis
Timothy Keller
Alister McGrath
Alvin Plantinga
James Sire
John Stackhouse
Lee Strobel
Richard Swinburne
N. T. Wright
Ravi Zacharias

Notes

Chapter 1

Dante's theory of reproduction

Dante, *Inferno*, "Purgatorio," Canto 25.

"We don't know where it came from."

"Big Bang Theory: An Overview," All About Science, accessed December 9, 2015, www.big-bang-theory.com.

"spherically symmetrical universe with Earth at the center, and you cannot disprove it based on observation."

W. Wayt Gibbs, "Profile George F. R. Ellis: Thinking Globally, Acting Universally," *Scientific American* 273, no. 4 (October 1995): 55.

Steven Weinberg claims that the Being that emerges from scientific investigation should be called an "abstract principle of order and harmony."

"Stephen Hawking's God," Counterbalance Foundation, accessed May 20, 2015, pbs.org/faithandreason/intro/cosmohaw-frame.html.

"Charles Birch, an Australian biologist, . . . [says] 'I find meaning in it.' "

"Purpose," Counterbalance Foundation, accessed May 20, 2015, pbs.org /faithandreason/intro/purpo-frame.html.

Chapter 2

"Life is not a primarily a quest for pleasure, as Freud believed..."

Harold S. Kushner, foreword to Victor Frankl, *Man's Search for Meaning* (Boston: Austrian ed., 1946; Boston: Beacon, 1959, 2006).

Wayne Booth, *The Rhetoric of Fiction* (Chicago: University of Chicago Press, 1961), 298.

"Dopamine is associated with seeking."

Steve Marsh, "The Wonder Junkie, " *Delta Sky* (May 2013): 67–68.

Chapter 3

C. S. Lewis. *Surprised by Joy* (New York: Harcourt, Brace, & World, 1955), 226.

Chapter 4

"About this time there lived Jesus"

Josephus, *Jewish Antiquities,* trans. Louis H. Feldman (Loeb Classical Library), 18.3.3 §63. See www.josephus.org/testimonium.htm.

"Sam Harris, speaks of walking in Jesus' footsteps, too, around the Sea of Galilee."

Frank Bruni, "Between Godliness and Godlessness," *New York Times,* August 30, 2014, www.nytimes.com/2014/08/31/opinion/sunday/frank-bruni-between-godliness-and-godlessness.html?_r=o.

Chapter 5

"The Jewish spirit of YHWH roars like a wind..."

Jewish Encyclopedia.com, "Holy Spirit," accessed May 2, 2015, jewishencyclopedia.com/articles/7833-holy-spirit.

"a force too deep for the 'measure stick.'"

Samuel Allen, ed., *Poems from Africa* (New York: Thomas Y. Crowell Co., 1973), 23.

"Around 159,960 Christians are martyred for their faith every year."

Mary Fairchild, "Christianity Statistics: General Statistics and Facts About Christianity Today," About Religion and Spirituality, accessed August 19, 2015, christianity.about.com/od/denominations/p/christiantoday.htm.

"Jesuit Father Jose Gabriel Funes, who believes that God could easily have created other life forms."

Edward Pentin, "Alien Life Out There," *Catholic.net,* accessed May 20, 2015, www.catholic.net/index.php?option=dedestaca&id=410.

Chapter 6

"I see the church as a field hospital after battle."

Pope Francis, quoted in Antonio Spadaro, "A Big Heart Open to God," *America: The National Catholic Review,* September 30, 2013.

"not in the catacombs of Rome (although they did conduct burial services there)."

L. Michael White, "In the Catacombs," *Frontline,* accessed May 20, 2015, www.pbs.org./wgbh/pages/frontline/shows/religion/first/catacombs.html.

Chapter 7

"Houston, we have a problem."

From the movie *Apollo 13,* directed by Ron Howard, released June 30, 1995. (The original quote was from astronaut Jack Swigert, "Houston, we've had a problem here," on the Apollo 13 mission).

Chapter 8

"Sin is a great thing as long as it's recognized."

Flannery O'Connor, *A Prayer Journal* (New York: Farrar, Straus and Giroux, 2013), 26.

"Karl Menninger wrote a book about how the word *sin* simply vanished."

Karl A. Menninger, *Whatever Became of Sin* (New York: Hawthorn Books, 1973).

"One's real life is almost always the life one doesn't lead."

James Patterson and Howard Roughan, *Honeymoon* (New York: Grand Central Publishing, 2007), 271.

"John Donne preached as one who knew by experience the slipperiness of habitual sin."

Elizabeth Gray Vining, *Take Heed of Loving Me* (Philadelphia and New York: J. B. Lippincott, 1964), 5.

Chapter 10

"Stripped to a scream, undressed to a cry of pain..."

Karl Marlantes, *Matterhorn* (New York: Atlantic Monthly Press with El León Literary Arts, 2010), 399.

Chapter 11

"The sense of death is most in apprehension."

William Shakespeare, *Measure for Measure,* Act III, Scene 1.

"Though he slay me, yet will I trust him." Job 13:15, alternate translation in footnote to verse.

Acknowledgments

I'D LIKE TO THANK MY HUSBAND, Stockton, for his support, insights, encouragement, and endurance in bearing with me during the research, writing, and publishing process of this book. A huge thank you goes to my agent, Kathleen Niendorff, for being a friend as well as a colleague, and the team at Abingdon has also been excellent to work with, especially Jamie Chavez, Cat Hoort, Ramona Richards, and the proof readers as well as Lil Copan, who now works for Eerdmans. Several friends have read and given me wonderful suggestions for improving the manuscript: Sylvia Benitez, Anne Albritton, Bobby and Kathleen Ulich, and my husband, Stockton. I would also like to thank Yale Divinity School for allowing me to be a Fellow and use their library and the Overseas Ministry Study Center for letting me be a part of their community as I was writing the book.

About the Author

DR. LESLIE WILLIAMS HAS BEEN AN English professor at Midland College for more than twenty years, and a three-time Fellow of Yale University. She has written a number of books, including *Night Wrestling* (Finalist for the ECPA Gold Medallion) and *The Judas Conspiracy* (Honorable Mention for the Eric Hoffer Award) and a biography of Thomas Cranmer, to be published as part of Eerdmans' Library of Religious Biography Series in 2016. She lives in Kerrville, Texas, with her husband, Stockton Williams, rector of St. Peter's Episcopal Church, and enjoys spending time with her children and grandchildren, also living in Kerrville.